The Marvellous Connections Between ESG and Taxation

The Marvellous Connections Between ESG and Taxation

How Can Taxes Contribute to a More Sustainable World

Luis Wolf Trzcina

Wolters Kluwer

Published by:
Kluwer Law International B.V.
PO Box 316
2400 AH Alphen aan den Rijn
The Netherlands
E-mail: lrs-sales@wolterskluwer.com
Website: www.wolterskluwer.com/en/solutions/kluwerlawinternational

Sold and distributed by:
Wolters Kluwer Legal & Regulatory U.S.
920 Links Avenue
Landisville, PA 17538
United States of America
E-mail: customer.service@wolterskluwer.com

ISBN 978-94-035-0609-8

e-Book: ISBN 978-94-035-0619-7
web-PDF: ISBN 978-94-035-0629-6

Table of Contents

Introduction

I am a 49-year-old man, the son of a Holocaust survivor and a resilient Brazilian woman, both of whom instilled in me the value of kindness toward all, regardless of background. In January 2024, I lost my 50-year-old sister with special needs, who first taught me to view the world through the lens of diversity.

I was born and raised in Rio de Janeiro, where I spent most of my life and earned my three degrees—Law, Economics, and Accounting. I also had the opportunity to work and study in the United States (U.S.) for three years, which allowed me to develop new professional and personal skills. I am grateful to KPMG for the opportunity to live abroad as an expatriate executive during this time.

My journey with KPMG began in 2007, and I became a tax partner in 2014. By 2021, I had taken on the role of National Leader for ESG and Tax. My career, however, began in 1999 as a trainee at Arthur Andersen, which later merged with Deloitte.

Parallel to my professional career—and given that I hold a Tax Law master's degree from both Brazil and the U.S.—I also spent eight years as a professor at the Federal University of Rio de Janeiro. Currently, I am an MBA professor teaching "Risk Management and Due Diligence."

In April 2024, I released my first solo book, marking the beginning of a new journey as a writer, moving away from my role as a KPMG tax partner. This book explores the connections between Environmental, Social and Governance (ESG) and taxation, and to my delight, it reached #1 on Amazon's Brazil bestseller list in its category.

Following this success, Wolters Kluwer invited me to write a new book, which will dive deeper into the intersection of ESG and taxation from a global perspective. By the way, I would like to express my gratitude to my friend Loek Helderman for introducing me to the publishers at Wolters Kluwer.

While this book focuses on the tax incentives designed to achieve decarbonization, it also goes beyond by discussing purpose, authenticity, governance, the transition to a low-carbon economy, and the associated opportunities. It highlights the crucial role taxes can play in these processes.

Sustainability initiatives can create a healthier, fairer, and more prosperous world, directly contributing to human happiness and overall quality of life. That's exactly what this book is about, and how it can bring a sense of fulfillment—an "ikigai"—to us as tax professionals.

Important note: No political commentary will be made here. This is purely a positive and hopeful book about the times ahead.

CHAPTER 1

Purpose in Professional Life

a THE CONCEPT OF IKIGAI AND VIKTOR FRANKL'S IDEAS ON MEANING AND PURPOSE

Studying happiness is the subject of countless books, quotes, sayings and courses all around the world. It is also taken seriously by governments and organizations such as the United Nations, which classifies happiness through the World Happiness Report, an annual publication that ranks countries based on how happy their citizens perceive themselves to be.[1]

In a similar manner, Netflix's documentary "Blue Zones" is based on the idea popularized by the journalist and researcher Dan Buettner in the early 2000s, aiming to identify and study determined areas of the world where people tend to live significantly happier, longer and healthier lives compared to the global average.

In the words presented on the Netflix website itself to describe the documentary: "explorer and bestselling author Dan Buettner hosts an insightful adventure through longevity hotspots around the world." These five original Blue Zones—all of them described by the documentary, as well as in fascinating Buettner books (as, for example, "The Blue Zones: Lessons for Living Longer From the People Who've Lived the Longest"), are:

(1) Okinawa, Japan.
(2) Sardinia, Italy.
(3) Ikaria, Greece.
(4) Nicoya Peninsula, Costa Rica.
(5) Loma Linda, California, U.S.

1. This report is produced by the Sustainable Development Solutions Network and utilizes various data sources and methodologies to measure happiness, mainly a Gallup World Pool, which surveys people in over 150 countries. Its website is Home | The World Happiness Report, https://worldhappiness.report/.

These regions share common lifestyle characteristics, such as plant-based diets, regular physical activity, strong social connections and a sense of purpose.

Sense of purpose is constantly connected to happiness, and it is a powerful sentiment manifested when the Okinawa community is presented in the documentary. By the way, this feeling has a specific word in the Japanese language: "ikigai."

Ikigai is often translated as "what makes life worth living," i.e., having a purpose in life or "a reason for being." It is frequently used to describe what brings fulfillment, joy and meaning to life. The concept of ikigai involves finding a balance between four fundamental elements:

(1) What you love (Passion): Activities and pursuits that bring you joy and fulfillment.
(2) What you are good at (Profession): Skills and talents that you excel at and can offer to the world.
(3) What you can be paid for (Vocation): Skills, activities and a particular knowledge that can support you financially.
(4) What the world needs (Mission): Paths you can contribute to society and make a positive impact.

The intersection of these four elements represents "ikigai," the awesome spot where your passions, talents and financial livelihood align with the necessities of the world, leading to a profound and meaningful life.

Evidently, this concept is not only perceived by Japanese culture through the phenomenon of "ikigai." To not move so far, the other four communities mentioned as "blue zones" have an analogous lifestyle, also in some way based on purpose. Similarly, a *plan de vida*, or guiding life purpose, helps Nicoyans stay rationally and spiritually fulfilled to age 90 and beyond.

So, a positive reason to live is the key to keeping these senior citizens alive in the five blue zones (and wherever on the planet).

Like ikigai, which centers on finding a balance between personal passions, skills, and societal needs, Viktor Frankl's ideas in Logotherapy emphasize the pursuit of meaning, especially through purpose and resilience in the face of hardship.

Frankl was a neurologist, psychiatrist, and Holocaust survivor who developed Logotherapy, a form of existential analysis that emphasizes finding meaning in life as the primary motivational force for living. It emphasizes the importance of self-transcendence, connecting with something more significant than oneself, and finding a positive impact in relationships and contributions to society and to the community.

Traditional (and Freudian) psychology is concerned with a journey towards the past and the shady, unconscious mysteries all of us hold. Evidently, there are times when this is the proper approach to be taken; nevertheless, it treats problems as something relatively like a disease to be cured. In opposition to this approach, Frankl once wrote, "Logotherapy declares war on pathologism" because of his orientation targeting the future and the trust that humans have the true potential to move beyond inner and outer obstacles.

Frankl, born in Wien in 1905, wrote *Man's Search For Meaning*, a work that remains one of the most influential books of modern times. It is not a long book, and it does not use too much psychological or medical jargon. So, it is friendly reading, even for the ones who are not exactly touched by these studies.

The book's background is centered on Frankl's collapse from being a highly respected psychiatrist—who had already established a successful career, along with the school of Logotherapy and a family—to a person who had everything taken away from him because of the Holocaust. Under this sorrowful scenario, the easiest thing would be to give up all hope and wait for his own end.

As a resilience strategy during the times he was imprisoned, Frankl kept a manuscript with him, something he hoped to publish upon his release. He did it because he needed a project, something to give meaning to his life, even under so much suffering experience in concentration camps. And he needed to stay resilient.

The concept of resilience is first explained in the world of physics and engineering and means the property that certain materials can return to their original state after having received some kind of impact (the elasticity of a rubber band, for example). This idea shows us the need to change ourselves when we cannot change the circumstances around us.

Viktor Frankl's lessons on finding meaning and purpose can be deeply applicable in today's world, as they help individuals navigate personal and professional challenges, improve mental health and their focus, and enhance overall well-being. For Frankl, meaning can be found in various aspects of life, such as relationships, communities, or even suffering. He argued that having a sense of purpose allows people to endure hardships and challenges.

Frankl's ideas can also be applied to the workplace by encouraging individuals to seek meaningful and purposeful work. This can lead to increased job satisfaction, engagement, and productivity. And it is something that will be explored further in this book.

His ideas and the ikigai concept have many connections, but I would like to highlight their linked thoughts about resilience: it lies in someone's attitude to life and to his/her own difficulties, which is what determines your ability to cope with almost anything. So, the right attitude is an option, and it means not giving up by continuing to hope and believe that your past experiences do not have to determine your future.

This belief is crucial when someone experiences the death of loved ones (as Frankl experienced) or when a long life is lived (as Japanese people in Okinawa) and consequently undergoes the loss of family members, friends, and peers, which can lead to feelings of loneliness and grief.

And to find meaning depends on each of us life's story and can happen in several manners: by working on an idea that moves us, by loving/taking care of someone, by fostering meaningful relationships, by providing support in our communities and by developing a sense of belonging, among others. The common idea is to reframe complex times and adversities as opportunities for personal growth and self-discovery.

b ALIGNMENT WITH PERSONAL VALUES

As just mentioned, according to Victor Frankl's ideas, a positive attitude before adversities is an option, and it is fulfilled with trust in a better future. In his own words, as per his seminal book "Man's Search for Meaning":

> A positive attitude enables a person to endure suffering and disappointment as well as enhance enjoyment and satisfaction. A negative attitude intensifies pain and deepens disappointments; it undermines and diminishes pleasure, happiness, and satisfaction; it may even lead to depression or physical illness.

And it takes action: to be unhappy is an effortless way of living, as it does not require courage, effort or commitment. True achievement resides in the constant struggle to be happy, an ability to be continuously worked at—like everything valuable in life.

Stress, anxiety, negativity biases, social media comparisons and unresolved issues are passive behaviors that do not require so much to occupy our minds. It is illustrative to remember an old song played by Nirvana, which says, "I miss the comfort in being sad."[2] The comfortable thing to do is the lazy attitude.

But the comfortable thing is not the right attitude: to be mindful and grateful, to help others, to keep a healthy lifestyle and to engage in activities that provide a sense of purpose need a lot of dedication through a conscious effort and discipline that can make happiness become more achievable.

Having said that, work can be a major source of happiness, if it is joyful and meaningful. This is not the usual definition adopted by common sense when it is asked to define "very successful people," i.e., rich people.

Charles Duhigg, a Pulitzer Prize-winning journalist and the author of "The Power of Habit," brilliantly described this mistaken common sense at The New York Times magazine[3] in an article adequately named "America's professional elite: wealthy, successful and miserable."

Focusing only on money can lead to accepting jobs that offer high pay but little personal satisfaction. Also, focusing solely on earning money can lead to neglecting personal affection, relationships, hobbies, and overall well-being. This imbalance can lead to feelings of isolation, loneliness, and frustration.

Therefore, work does not have to be merely about money. Many people find fulfillment in their tasks through meaningful work, positive relationships with colleagues, and contributing to a larger purpose. When these elements are present, work can become a source of joy rather than stress.

Example? The attitude of unpaid volunteers towards their tasks easily demonstrates a more real accomplishment and joy than billionaires doing their "dream job."

Teachers, who are aware of their importance to the community, as they function as personal and social developers of future citizens and professionals, are inspirational

2. The name of the song is "Frances Farmer will have her revenge on Seattle."
3. America's Professional Elite: Wealthy, Successful and Miserable—The New York Times (nytimes.com), https://www.nytimes.com/interactive/2019/02/21/magazine/elite-professionals-jobs-happiness.html.

models and play a crucial role in providing more equitable educational opportunities, helping to bridge gaps caused by socioeconomic discrepancies.

Also, teachers often serve as mentors, offering guidance and support beyond the classroom. Therefore, the importance of being a teacher lies in their profound and lasting impact on individuals and society, as they shape minds, instill values, inspire innovation, and contribute to the development of a knowledgeable, ethical, and compassionate society.

Amy Wrzesniewski, a professor of organizational behavior at the Yale School of Management, is known for her research on work, motivation, and meaning, particularly regarding how people perceive and experience their jobs. Jointly with her colleagues, she identified three primary ways people can orient themselves toward their work. These directions reflect how individuals perceive the purpose of their jobs:

- Job Orientation: People with this orientation see work primarily as a means to an end, such as earning money to support their personal life or interests outside of work.
- Career Orientation: These individuals focus on advancement, achievement, and gaining higher status or recognition within their profession.
- Calling Orientation: For these people, work is inherently meaningful, and they see it as a source of personal fulfillment and a way to contribute to society or a greater purpose.

Wrzesniewski found that individuals who see their work as a calling are generally more satisfied and engaged, as they feel their work has intrinsic value. However, individuals can shift between these orientations depending on their circumstances and how they craft their jobs.[4]

Several work activities can contribute to personal happiness—besides volunteer work and teachers—mainly if they are connected to the alignment of personal and work values, thus creating a fulfilling and harmonious professional life. For instance, Amy Wrzesniewski discovered that hospital janitors who filled their work with meaning and made connections to patients were much happier with their jobs than those who did not follow the same path.

Similarly to the ikigai concept, the track towards happiness involves identifying personal values (what really matters to you), a wise choice of employer (by looking for companies whose mission, vision, and values resonate with yours), fostering positive workplace relationships (by surrounding yourself with colleagues who share similar values and seeking mentors who embody the values you respect) and a regular reflection and reassessment if your work environment continues to align with your values.

Imagine someone who is passionate about nature, environmental conservation and the intricacies of how ecosystems function. He or she might start a career in a

4. Do You Have a Job, Career or Calling? The Difference Matters (forbes.com), https://www.forbes.com/sites/melodywilding/2018/04/23/do-you-have-a-job-career-or-calling-the-difference-matters/.

traditional corporate job, in a conventional office, under a 9 to 5 schedule. Then, he or she eventually transitions to a role in a sustainability-focused organization, where this professional can move into a leadership position, driving sustainable practices within the company and influencing industry standards. Consequently, by aligning career and passion for the environment, deeper satisfaction and a sense of accomplishment will naturally be achieved.

Note these concepts will be extended in Chapter 1 section d, but in any case, aligning personal values with work values involves self-awareness, proactive communication, and continuous reflection. By taking deliberate steps to ensure alignment, greater satisfaction and success can be achieved in professional life.

Bringing it to our personal lives, the purpose is what moves us and drives us forward, whether it is something vast (going into politics in order to provide better life conditions to a community, being a scientist who is researching a new treatment for an illness) or more personal (taking care of elder parents, children, teaching some skill in the community or doing volunteer work).

Taking care of older relatives, for instance, can be challenging and demanding, but overall, it constitutes a worthwhile experience, both for the caregiver and the relative being cared for, as it comprises: (i) reciprocity and gratitude: it is a sense of duty to care for their elders who once cared for them, in the way of giving back their love and support; (ii) respect for elders: caring for elders can be a way of demonstrating love and appreciation for their wisdom, experience, and contributions to the family and society; and (iii) keep connections active: caring for an elderly relative can help strengthen emotional ties and maintain a sense of connection within the family, as well as the personal fulfillment in helping their loved ones and making a positive impact on their lives.

Realizing the purpose of life is a genuinely introspective and personal journey that can be approached in various ways and that involves the discovery of core values. Life's calling is what makes you feel that life is significant and goes beyond a mere job or career and encompasses a sense of fulfillment and contribution to something larger than oneself.

This idea is fully associated with ikigai and Frankl's ideas, as well as the next section of this chapter, where we will talk about working for a cause.

c CONTRIBUTION TO A GREATER CAUSE

A big part of job satisfaction is being truly engaged with the company you work for and enjoying your professional activities daily. But when you combine your technical skills with a cause you care deeply about, you can take this passion to a whole new level.

Working with a cause means engaging in professional activities that are driven by a larger purpose than financial gain or personal achievement. It involves linking your work with a mission or set of values that aim to create positive social, environmental, or cultural impact, and it will usually involve:

(1) Meaningful impact
Your work contributes to a larger mission that you are passionate about, such as improving healthcare, promoting education, protecting the environment, or advocating for social justice and reducing inequalities gap (such as the previously mentioned activities performed by teachers). It is based on a deep-seated belief in the cause, which can lead to a more fulfilling and rewarding work experience.

(2) Authenticity
As your personal values are aligned with the goals and values of the cause, it leads to a sense of coherence and integrity in your professional life. So, you will bring your whole self to work, as your actions and efforts reflect your core beliefs. And it means to be authentic.

(3) Positive work environment
You work alongside others who share your passion for the cause through the same goals, as the work aims to address societal challenges and contribute to the well-being of others.

Examples of Working with a Cause

- Nonprofit Organizations: Working for nonprofits that address issues like people with special needs, poverty, animal welfare, or disaster relief.
- Social Enterprises: Engaging in business ventures that prioritize social impact (e.g., endowment foundations) alongside financial returns.
- Public Service: Serving in government or public sector roles that aim to improve community services, public health, or education.
- Advocacy and Activism: Working with organizations or movements that advocate for policy changes, social justice, or environmental protection.

Note that under the examples above, the hours dedicated will usually be non-remunerated or will be worked under a low remuneration. Consequently, it may usually function as a part-time job together with a "regular" job.

But there are good reasons to believe in a better future for capitalism and to spend hours for a great cause while working on a "regular" job: it has to do with Corporate Social Responsibility (CSR) companies.

More and more, CSR is a reality of capitalism. And it means a business model that helps a company be socially accountable to itself, its stakeholders, and the public, as well as environmentally responsible. Being a CSR is a strategy usually employed by large corporations, bearing in mind the fact that their visibility implies the necessity of setting standards of ethical behavior for their peers, competition and the industry.

An example of CSR companies is the ones which are considered B Corps, i.e., for-profit companies that meet specific social and environmental performance standards, accountability, and transparency criteria. They are certified by B Lab, a nonprofit organization that verifies a company's impact in areas like governance, workers, community, environment, and customers. B Corps legally commit to balancing profit and purpose.

Under this new corporate mindset, these companies *are not* nonprofit (in reality, various of them are highly profitable), and at the same time, they work on ways to create social and environmental benefits while chasing organizational aims, such as revenue growth and maximizing shareholder value.

On the flip side, while CSR initiatives can significantly enhance a company's reputation and operations, some companies engage in "greenwashing" or "social washing," where they falsely advertise ethical practices without substantive action. This has led to growing skepticism among consumers, who now demand greater transparency and accountability.

In any event, to be CSR brings several benefits for companies, such as: *enhanced reputation and consumer loyalty* (companies known for their CSR efforts often enjoy a better reputation and stronger brand loyalty among consumers), *employee satisfaction*, as a strong CSR program can improve employee morale, retention, and attract talent who value ethical and socially responsible employers and a *more accurate risk management*, by proactively addressing social and environmental issues can help mitigate risks and ensure long-term sustainability.

Working in a CSR can lead people to work with a cause and to dedicate professional efforts to something greater than themselves, aligning their work with their values and striving to make a positive impact on society or the environment. And do it all in a "regularly paid" job.

Having said that, I would like to bring an example of a CSR company: Best Buy—the U.S. multinational consumer electronics retailer.

Best Buy was recognized by an independent institution named Ethisphere that annually appoints the designation for the world's most ethical companies.[5]

Best Buy's business case is a demonstration of how a company can turn challenges into opportunities in a market where its top competitor (Amazon) offers several advantages, including a wider range of available products as well as habitually lower prices due to its massive scale and efficiencies, which can make it difficult for Best Buy to compete on price.

It is impressive to read an article prepared in 2021 by Best Buy CEO (Hubert Joly) at Harvard Business Review (whose title is "Creating a Meaningful Corporate Purpose")[6] and to notice how close the company's purpose is connected to Ikigai concept:

> To land on a meaningful, authentic, credible, and powerful purpose, explore all four circles thoroughly. Here are some factors to consider:
>
> > What the world needs: What specific, important unmet needs exist in the world? How critical is it to address these needs? What difference will it make?
> > What people at the company are passionate about: What drives people at the company? What difference are they keen to make in the world? (These apply to senior leadership as well as the overall employee population.)

5. Please find the full 2024 by Ethisphere at: Ethisphere Announces the 2024 World's Most Ethical Companies—Ethisphere | Good. Smart. Business. Profit.®, https://ethisphere.com/ethisphere-announces-the-2024-worlds-most-ethical-companies/.
6. Creating a Meaningful Corporate Purpose (hbr.org), https://hbr.org/2021/10/creating-a-meaningful-corporate-purpose.

> What the company is uniquely good at: What are the unique assets that allow it to address certain needs in a way others can't? How do they need to evolve/be augmented to address the chosen needs in a way others aren't?
> How the company can create economic value: What business opportunities stem from these considerations? How attractive are the associated potential profit pools? Can the company capture enough of this value?

Hence, Best Buy used its potential weakness (to be a brick and mortar, i.e., a traditional street-side business that offers products and services to its customers face-to-face) to transform it into a strength, calling it a "human touch" for technology, aiming for a personalized customer service, by a team named "Geek Squad," that provides services in-store and 24-hour telephone and emergency on-site support.

This objective of providing this "human touch" is clear in company's purpose statement:[7]

> At Best Buy, our purpose is to enrich lives through technology. We do that by leveraging our unique combination of tech expertise and human touch to meet our customers' everyday needs, whether they come to us online, visit our stores or invite us into their homes. We have more than 1,000 stores and more than 90,000 employees in the United States and Canada.

Besides Ethisphere, another independent research company provides ranks on corporate ethics and reputation is the Global RepTrak 100, through an intelligence platform that provides measures of how stakeholders feel, think, and act towards a given company.

In their annual 2024 report, LEGO Group was ranked as the most reputable company in the world for the second consecutive year.[8] It not only has to do with all the efforts made by LEGO Group to "inspire and develop the builders of tomorrow," as said in its mission statement but also is linked to all the efforts to phase out single-use plastic packaging for its bricks with all packaging to be sustainable by 2025.

Chief Executive Officer of the LEGO Group, Niels B. Christiansen, said:[9] "I am very proud the LEGO Group has been named the World's Most Reputable Company again in 2024. This is testament to the dedication of our colleagues who all play a part in building a sustainable future and a better world for our children to inherit. Together, we're working to create positive, lasting impact and inspiring the builders of tomorrow."

Plenty of corporations have clear, engaging and actionable mission statements, building it as a relevant part of a strategic planning process, as it comprises a summary of the "why" behind a brand. Please find below some examples:

> American Express: "To become essential to our customers by providing differentiated products and services to help them achieve their aspirations."

7. About Best Buy—Best Buy Corporate News and Information, https://corporate.bestbuy.com/about-best-buy/.
8. RepTrak 2024—About Us—LEGO.com, https://www.lego.com/en-us/aboutus/news/2024/april/reptrak-2024.
9. RepTrak 2024—About Us—LEGO.com, https://www.lego.com/en-us/aboutus/news/2024/april/reptrak-2024.

> Google: "Organize the world's information and make it universally accessible and useful."
>
> IKEA: "To offer a wide range of well-designed, functional home furnishing products at prices so low that as many people as possible will be able to afford them."
>
> Microsoft: "To empower every person and every organization on the planet to achieve more."
>
> Nike: "Bring inspiration and innovation to every athlete in the world. If you have a body, you are an athlete."
>
> TED: "Spread ideas."

Of course, things are not so positive, as many brands are being accused of malpractices, such as greenwashing and social washing, i.e., misuse that takes some companies to fake their sustainability and social purpose claims, thus leading to a feeling of inauthenticity.

Connected to this feeling, the next topic will cover something not so constructive: a toxic work environment.

d WORK ENVIRONMENT

Toxic workplace cultures have plenty of gossip, animosity, cliques, mistrust, and selfishness. Dysfunction arises in this environment full of negative attitudes, disrespect, show-off, power battles, poor communication, and abusive leadership. This overall panorama leads to a decrease in creativity, teamwork and, of course, the quality and the quantity of production. In parallel, there is a growth in manipulation, rumors, blame, and fear. Inappropriate jokes and comments are also part of this unpleasant recipe.

All of which causes employees to become less loyal and emotionally devastated. And these hostile working conditions may trigger overwhelming fatigue, negative attitudes or a lack of commitment to clients and dissatisfaction with job performance. All these conditions together characterize job burnout, a syndrome resulting from such chronic stress at work. This process may lead to unwanted effects on workers themselves, their families, their peers and the corporations' environments.

As the "cancel culture" is globally spreading, it also includes criticism of the workplace, which is highly notable in online platforms like Glassdoor, which allow anonymity to provide honest feedback from current or former employees.

For example, the retail company Abercrombie & Fitch faced significant backlash and "cancellation" primarily due to controversies related to its branding, marketing strategies, and company culture, which were perceived as exclusionary and discriminatory. Social media played a crucial role in amplifying the hostile response against Abercrombie & Fitch. Negative stories, controversies, and criticisms spread quickly online, leading to calls for boycotts and further tarnishing the brand's image.

Or, as said by "The New Yorker":[10]

> In 2004, the company agreed to pay fifty million dollars to several thousand employees in order to settle a class-action lawsuit charging that it discriminated against African-Americans, Latinos, and Asian-Americans in both its hiring practices and its advertising. Among other things, the suit alleged that non-whites were regularly shoehorned into back-of-the-store jobs where customers wouldn't see them as much.

Abercrombie & Fitch has been working on rebranding and repositioning itself in recent years by embracing more inclusive and diverse marketing, redesigning its stores, and focusing on digital channels. A quote from current CEO Fran Horowitz on its website says: "Abercrombie isn't a brand where you need to fit in—it's one where everyone truly belongs." However, the legacy of its past issues has made the road to recovery challenging.

In addition to all these relevant topics on diversity and inclusion, more than ever, frustrated workers are leaving their jobs without securing another one. For many, being unemployed is not as harmful to their mental health as the possibility of continuing in terrible employment.

As expressed by the World Economic Forum:[11]

> We've all experienced stressful situations in the workplace. From unrealistic performance expectations to demanding bosses or strong personalities, few are free of the work-related pressures that can impact mental health.
>
> The average person spends 90,000 hours or roughly one-third of their life at work. As a result, the environment, stress levels and interpersonal dynamics can majorly impact workers' mental health and well-being.
>
> At any given time, more than one in 10 workers are absent due to anxiety, depression or burnout. Beyond the interpersonal, balancing the demands of work and life, managing health issues and the ever-rising cost of living can all be amplifying stressors.

On the opposite side we are born with a desire to explore, experiment, and learn. In fact, part of our brain has a "seeking system" that rewards us for engaging in these new activities and feeling wired to find motivation and learning. This "seeking system" releases dopamine—a neurotransmitter that fuels our motivation—through the exact attributes set above: exploration, experimentation, and learning.

This natural feeling arises because we fall engaged when we grow, improve, learn and navigate to be the best version of ourselves. And the question is: how can someone push you to succeed and reach your full potential at work?

The answer, again, is *purpose*, as it plays a crucial role in enhancing the work environment. It can manifest in some paths in the professional life:

---

10. Abercrombie's Legal Defeat—and Its Cultural Failure | The New Yorker, https://www.newyorker.com/news/daily-comment/abercrombie-fitch-samantha-elauf-discrimination-supreme-court.
11. Workers' mental health and well-being need a holistic approach | World Economic Forum (weforum.org), https://www.weforum.org/agenda/2024/05/how-to-transform-workplace-mental-health-through-a-holistic-approach-to-employee-health-and-well-being/.

- To understand how your work affects others: for example, if you work as an auditor—i.e., a professional responsible for reviewing and verifying an organization's financial records to ensure compliance with regulatory standards and internal policies—the tasks proposed sometimes sound too repetitive and monotonous. However, there is a bigger picture on this because auditors' work provides transparency in an organization's financial reporting and then helps maintain stakeholder confidence, supports regulatory compliance, and enhances overall business efficiency. So, this is the purpose of these apparently repetitive and monotonous tasks.
- Adequately rewarding people in the workplace involves recognizing and appreciating their contributions in ways that are meaningful and motivating to them. Effective rewards can boost morale, enhance job satisfaction, and improve overall performance. These rewards can be monetary (e.g., salary increase, bonus, stock options) or non-monetary (e.g., public acknowledgement, awards and certificates).
- To set a positive standard through your own actions and serve as a role model for your team or organization, i.e., leading by example by truly demonstrating the behaviors, attitudes, and work ethics that you expect from your peers, bosses and team.
- To provide consistent and constructive feedback to help the team understand how to improve their performance and the areas for development, as well as foster a culture of open communication where everyone feels heard and valued and capable of having autonomy and power to make decisions related to their tasks.

Patagonia, the outdoor clothing and gear company, is well recognized for integrating purpose into its business model. The company highlights environmental responsibility, social activism, and sustainable practices by asserting in its statement of purpose[12] that the company:

> Examine our practices openly and honestly, learn from our mistakes and meet our commitments. We value integrity in both senses: that our actions match our words (we walk the talk), and that all of our work contributes to a functional whole (our sum is greater than our parts).

Also the purpose is also a crucial part of this statement, as it is expressed as a core value of the desire to:

> Build the best product, provide the best service and constantly improve everything we do. The best product is useful, versatile, long-lasting, repairable and recyclable. Our ideal is to make products that give back to the Earth as much as they take.

Patagonia really encourages customers to repair and reuse their products rather than replace them. They offer a "Worn Wear" program, which facilitates the trade, repair, and recycling of used Patagonia gear, as "85% of clothing ends up in landfills or

12. Our Core Values—Patagonia, https://www.patagonia.com/core-values/.

gets incinerated. One of the best things we can do for the planet is keep stuff in use longer and reduce our overall consumption. That means buying less, repairing more and trading in gear when you no longer need it."[13]

Going beyond, Patagonia's founder, Yvon Chouinard, has transferred ownership of the firm to a trust fund committed to fighting climate change.

Patagonia is indeed a purpose-driven company. However, note that this practice is spreading more and more in the corporate world. This welcome scenario is fully connected to Environmental, Social, and Governance (ESG) principles.

Directly speaking, ESG can bring more purpose to work by aligning business practices with values that prioritize sustainability, social responsibility, and ethical governance. And consequently, dodging all the toxic practices mentioned at the beginning of this section.

This alignment can enhance employee engagement, attract talent, and create a positive impact on society and the environment. And create a lot of opportunities for everyone who is prepared to embrace it.

e CONTINUOUS LEARNING AND GROWTH

When the Industrial Revolution erupted in the late 18th century, a group formed by English workmen named "Luddites" started to destroy laborsaving machinery as a protest against automated production. They sabotaged equipment and smashed the machines they believed had taken or threatened their jobs.

Members of the group claimed to be followers of the legendary General Ludd (a folkloric character) whose name was used as a nickname in threatening letters to factory owners and government officials, whose private properties were often attacked too.

This story gives us a historical perspective on the continuous battle between labor and technology and highlights how uncertain the times after a technological disruption are, mainly when it shall change the way people habitually work and live.

This conflict between the old and the new is still very relevant in today's fast-changing economic world. Even when technology helps the economy overall, there will be losers, and they may fight back, aiming to make the old regime resist.

Currently, there is a disseminated fear about artificial intelligence (AI)'s potential to displace jobs in the years ahead, as it may be a reason for laying off workers and rethinking new hires in the near future. So, a potential "new luddite" would argue that AI is a job destructor. Conversely, some experts say that AI and machine learning will help workers by establishing more occupations than they replace.

In any case—and looking on the bright side of the green agenda—it is important to quote an extract from an article published on the World Economic Forum website:[14]

---

13. Used Patagonia® Clothing & Gear | Worn Wear—Patagonia Worn Wear®, https://wornwear.patagonia.com/.
14. Future of jobs is green: Climate change is changing labour markets | World Economic Forum (weforum.org), https://www.weforum.org/agenda/2023/04/future-of-jobs-is-green-2023-climate-change-labour-markets/.

> Countries around the world have set ambitious targets to reach net zero by 2050—requiring a seismic shift across global economies and industries to change the way we do things. Both governments and businesses are looking hard at how to drive this green transition further and faster. Governments are setting the national direction and organizations are reinventing their business models in order to play their part. The good news is that we are seeing this progress reflected in hiring for green jobs. (...)
>
> But make no mistake—the green job revolution is much broader than hiring sustainability managers. Be it engineers who can build and run wind farms or managers who can help make the day-to-day running of a business more sustainable, we need to see a rapid scale-up in roles that require green skills if we want real change.

Therefore, "green jobs" are on the rise, as investments in the energy transition will be very positive for job creation, depending on the availability of qualified professionals. So, climate change is reshaping the workforce, as the ESG standards and their extensive application will require new skills.

These ESG standards (especially focusing on the environmental aspect of ESG) can play a significant role in job creation in several ways:

(1) Renewable Energy: The move towards renewable energy sources such as solar, wind, biomass and hydroelectric power creates jobs in manufacturing, installation, conservation, and research and development. These sectors often demand a local workforce, lifting employment in areas where these projects are executed. Also, renewable energy acts as a massive job creator, producing higher energy per unit than conventional sources. It is an outcome of longer and more diverse supply chains, higher labor intensity, and increased net profit margins.

(2) Sustainable Practices in Traditional Industries: Implementing sustainable practices—such as compliance with environmental law, energy efficiency, waste management, and sustainable sourcing—in traditional industries like manufacturing, agriculture, and construction can also lead to the creation of new job roles.

(3) Innovation and R&D: Companies observing ESG frequently invest in research and development to create innovative answers for environmental and social challenges. This drives the need for a skilled workforce in the science and technology fields in order to create more sustainable and carbon-neutral products and services, thus transforming processes at each step of the value chain.

(4) Circular Economy: The transition to a circular economy, which emphasizes recycling, reusing, and minimizing waste, creates jobs in recycling facilities, repair and refurbishment services, and product design for sustainability. Innovation in their production processes is also crucial for a circular economy, as it designs products for more prolonged use, jointly with reuse strategies. As a result, companies increase their operational efficiency and cost-effectiveness.

So, by fostering a business environment that leads to sustainability, ESG principles can stimulate economic growth and job creation across different manners. Preparing for these jobs comprises a combination of education, skills, and experience that may be obtained through:

- Formal education: Pursue degrees in fields such as environmental science, sustainability, social sciences, public policy, business administration, accounting, law or finance with a focus on ESG principles. Also, certifications in ESG-specific areas, such as sustainable finance, CSR, environmental management, or social impact assessment. Organizations like the Global Reporting Initiative (GRI) and the Sustainability Accounting Standards Board offer significant courses for these abilities.
- Professional experience, internships and volunteering with organizations that have strong ESG practices, like NGOs, social enterprises, sustainability consulting firms, or companies with robust CSR programs. A notable initiative was adopted by an organization named Fashion Revolution that claims a clean, safe, fair, transparent and accountable fashion industry. On its website, it is stated that:[15] "the colossal carbon impact of clothing happens at every stage of the fashion supply chain and product life cycle, but 70% of fashion's emissions originate from upstream activities such as raw material production and processing. Despite this, most major brands still fail to take basic steps towards environmental due diligence at their supplier sites."
- Networking: to join professional associations and networks focused on ESG, such as the International Society of Sustainability Professionals (ISSP) or the Global Impact Investment Network. Further, it is advisable to attend ESG conferences, workshops, and seminars to stay updated on industry trends, learn from experts, and build connections with professionals in the field.

By combining education, practical experience, networking, and continuous learning, it is possible to build a strong foundation for a successful career in ESG and contribute to the positive impact of these principles in various sectors. New opportunities demand new skills, and these new skills are capable of being achieved. Shifting to a low-carbon economy will unlock new jobs and opportunities.

Therefore, ESG and continuous learning are naturally linked, as the progressing nature of ESG demands lifelong adaptation, knowledge expansion, and personal growth. Whether through adapting to new regulations, embracing innovation, or improving social responsibility, the principles of ESG promote a mindset of lifelong learning that benefits both organizations and individuals.

Learning can be a route to something new, rewire our brains, and reinvent our futures. It can also be a source of happiness, as learning something new forces us to live in the moment and makes our brains better and younger.

Especially when the new ability learned has to do with purpose.

15. Taking action on fashion and the climate crisis: Fashion Revolution, https://www.fashionrevolution.org/climatecrisis/.

CHAPTER 2

ESG Development

a TRANSITION TO A LOW-CARBON ECONOMY

The Industrial Revolution marked a significant shift from an agrarian, handicraft-based economy to one dominated by industry and machine manufacturing. The introduction of technology created new ways of working and living and essentially transformed society.

Beyond the social aspects discussed earlier, such as the Luddites, the Industrial Revolution had a profound impact on energy consumption and the environment, since:

- It marked the beginning of large-scale use of fossil fuels, particularly coal, to power steam engines, factories, and later, transportation. The burning of these fuels released large amounts of carbon dioxide (CO_2) and other greenhouse gases (GHGs) (such as methane, nitrous oxide and sulfur dioxide) into the atmosphere.
- To make way for urban development and to provide raw materials for industries, vast forest areas were cleared. Trees absorb CO_2 during photosynthesis, which makes them important carbon sinks. Therefore, their removal reduced Earth's capacity to sequester carbon, increasing atmospheric CO_2 levels.
- The Industrial Revolution spurred substantial population growth due to improved living standards and medical advancements. More people meant higher energy consumption and greater environmental impact.

Until the Industrial Revolution, the balance between the carbon in the world's forests and in the atmosphere remained constant, as demonstrated by samples of CO_2 confined in ice during the past thousand years.

Preindustrial humans emitted small amounts of CO_2, mostly from fires and land clearance. However, it was the Industrial Revolution that significantly disrupted the carbon cycle.

CO_2 and other GHGs are responsible for keeping the planet's temperature in the ideal conditions for life as we know it today: this greenhouse effect makes the Earth pleasant for humans and other living beings that live on it.

However, with the imbalance triggered after the industrial times between the amount of gas emissions and the natural capacity that ecosystems absorb CO_2, the result started to trap heat in the atmosphere, acting as a blanket, thus leading to a rise in global average temperatures.

Note this perception is not something recent. Such imbalance was first noted in 1896 by a Swedish scientist named Svante Arrhenius—the first Swede to achieve the prestigious award from the Swedish Academy in 1903—who proposed that the burning of fossil fuels could lead to global warming due to an increase in CO_2 in the atmosphere. Arrhenius calculated that a doubling of atmospheric CO_2 could significantly increase Earth's surface temperature, a crucial definition to contemporary climate science.

This is often referred to as global warming, a major component of climate change. These higher global temperatures can lead to more extreme weather patterns, including heatwaves, droughts, heavier rainfall, and stronger hurricanes. Also, higher temperatures contribute to the melting of polar ice caps and glaciers, resulting in rising sea levels. This threatens coastal communities and ecosystems.

So, past industrial activities have set the stage for the challenges we are facing now:

> 2024, July 24th was the planet's hottest day ever, breaking a record set the day before. António Guterres, secretary general of the U.N., said that[1] "Extreme temperatures are no longer a one-day, one-week or one-month phenomenon. If there is one thing that unites our divided world, it's that we're all increasingly feeling the heat. Earth is becoming hotter and more dangerous for everyone, everywhere. (...) We know what is driving it: fossil fuel-charged, human-induced climate change and we know it is going to get worse."

Nevertheless, some scarce voices are rising against the idea of a relationship between the increase in GHG emissions and climate change. One of the most relevant is John F. Clauser, who shared the Nobel Prize in physics in 2022 and who said, "there is no climate crisis"[2]—a declaration that contradicts the overwhelming scientific agreement on the matter.

Of course, the purpose of this book is not to debate environmental science, but the fact is: capitalism has already started to move its attention to new alternatives using less carbon than we have been doing in the last two hundred years. The transition to a low-carbon economy will result in a massive reallocation of investment as energy systems are rewired, and it shall also be a coordinated effort between policy, technology, and consumer and investor preferences.

1. Earth's Hottest Days Ever—The New York Times (nytimes.com), https://www.nytimes.com/2024/07/25/climate/earths-hottest-days-ever.html.
2. John Clauser won a Nobel Prize. Then he started denying climate change—The Washington Post, https://www.washingtonpost.com/climate-environment/2023/11/16/john-clauser-nobel-climate-denial/.

So, now it is time to introduce one of the most cited people when the topic is reallocation of investment under this new corporate mindset: Larry Fink, the co-founder, chairman, and CEO of BlackRock. Fink has a remarkable journey in the finance world, and BlackRock manages an impressive USD 10 trillion in assets, which makes it the largest asset manager in the world. Just to make a trivial comparison, this amount corresponds to the double of Germany's gross domestic product and half of the Chinese one.

So, when BlackRock speaks, markets and organizations tend to listen.

Fink annually writes a letter to global CEOs, and it works as a compass for the business world. His 2020 letter[3] titled "A Fundamental Reshaping of Finance," is notable because it signaled a major shift in the financial industry's approach to climate change, sustainability, and corporate governance, setting pioneer standards and new expectations for businesses worldwide.

This letter addresses climate change as a significant factor that would redesign finance and make sustainability a core strategy by emphasizing its importance in investment strategies. Fink also urged companies to focus on long-term strategies rather than short-term profits, as he believed that long-term value creation should be at the forefront of corporate governance and business models. And it clearly involves considering decarbonization as a key element. In his own words:

> Over the next few years, one of the most important questions we will face is the scale and scope of government action on climate change, which will generally define the speed with which we move to a low-carbon economy.

Also, the letter echoed the idea that companies need to have a purpose beyond profit, which is essential for long-term success, as well as the notion of stakeholder capitalism, where the interests of all stakeholders, including employees, customers, and the communities in which companies operate, should be considered alongside shareholders' interests.

Climate change, social concerns and related governance issues will shift the long-term business environment. Forward-thinking business leaders—like Larry Fink—are taking action now to be ahead of the game, not only because this is the right thing to do but also to ensure their own survival, relevance and impact in the future.

Another leader who is worthy of citation is Paul Polman, former CEO at Unilever (2009-2019). Polman was central in embedding sustainability into the core of the company's operations and strategy, and he advocates long-term, stakeholder-focused capitalism, inspiring other businesses to adopt responsible, ethical practices. His efforts have contributed significantly to the mainstreaming of ESG principles in corporate governance, making him a central figure in the global ESG arena.

Just an important disclaimer before moving on: these socially conscious leaders who pursue high ESG standards are not labeled by any political stamp. And they give the impression they do not want it, as they are businesspeople, more interested in staying neutral and therefore avoid contributing to political polarization.

3. Available at Larry Fink's Letter to CEOs | BlackRock, https://www.blackrock.com/corporate/investor-relations/2020-larry-fink-ceo-letter.

Furthermore, a political classification of ESG is so perilous that Larry Fink has decided to stop utilizing this acronym when discussing this type of investment, albeit this change in language does not mean a shift in BlackRock's practices. Instead, Fink is currently using more specific terms, such as decarbonization and conscious capitalism.

As Time magazine explained:[4]

> Fink is not alone. As the backlash to ESG has grown over the last year, business leaders have changed the way they talk about their climate work to tiptoe around the political faultlines. Some have used different language that avoids phrases like ESG; others have avoided even talking about it in public venues. But in operational plans and corporate-strategy sessions investors and business executives in most industries say they haven't backtracked at all, particularly on environment- and climate-related issues.

Likewise, a survey carried out by KPMG by interviewing 1,325 CEOs around the world between July 25 and August 29, 2024, demonstrated that:[5]

> We're also seeing a growing level of politicization and polarization of issues such as social mobility and climate change, and it's creating challenges for CEOs who are already under pressure to meet or reassess established targets. As a result, some global CEOs are shifting how they communicate their ESG efforts. In this year's survey, 69 percent reveal that while they've retained the same climate related strategies over the last 12 months, they've adapted the language and terminology they use internally and externally to meet changing stakeholder needs. For example, political and social forces have pushed some businesses to change the language they use, with some organizations preferring to use general terminology such as "sustainability" over the more encompassing term of "ESG."

In fact, since 2022, the ESG movement has experienced criticism both in the U.S. and Europe by increasing backlash against green policies. Geopolitical events, including Russia's invasion of Ukraine, have expanded the demand for oil, which may run counter to activist pressures to phase out fossil fuel exploration.

In addition, the Heritage Foundation,[6] a conservative think-tank based in Washington, believes that "under the umbrella of ESG activism, corporations have become unimaginably woke." The Foundation advocates that CEOs should focus on profit and not allow capital to be diverted from the purposes for which the company was created. ESG, it argues, is value-destructive, politically motivated, and has a negative impact on investor returns.

Another dangerous practice for ESG is "greenwashing," i.e., the marketing tactic that companies use to deceive environmentally conscious customers when businesses entitle themselves as sustainable by providing wrong or misleading information about their practices.

---

4. Larry Fink Takes on ESG Backlash | TIME, https://time.com/6291317/larry-fink-esg-climate-action/.
5. KPMG 2024 CEO Outlook, https://kpmg.com/xx/en/our-insights/value-creation/kpmg-global-ceo-outlook-survey-2024.html#: ~ :text = The%2010th%20edition%20of%20the%20KPMG%20CEO%20Outlook.
6. The ESG Pushback | The Heritage Foundation, https://www.heritage.org/environment/heritage-explains/the-esg-pushback.

ESG endeavors are a journey, so bumps along the way are expected. No company is perfect, and some valid issues have been indeed raised about ESG, but the need for companies to recognize and address their externalities will remain crucial to maintaining their social license.

b INVESTORS AND SOCIAL PRESSURE

The term ESG was first brought to attention in 2004 in a report performed by a joint initiative of financial institutions and the United Nations, named as "Who Cares Wins."

"Environmental" refers to a company's commitment to sustainability and environmental issues. "Social" focuses on the corporative relationship with both internal and external stakeholders, including employees, customers, suppliers, and the whole community around. "Governance" encompasses the field of corporate governance like leadership, financial and legal integrity, compliance, audit, and shareholder rights.

As mentioned in the previous section, the acronym itself may be under scrutiny, but the core principles of corporate sustainability that strengthen ESG conducts are very alive and continue to be a significant trend in the financial world. ESG criteria are used by investors to screen potential investments based on a company's adherence to sustainable and ethical practices.

Many investors believe that companies with strong ESG practices are better positioned for long-term success, as these corporations are under stricter compliance rules. Corporations with robust ESG routines are a lot better prepared for potential regulatory changes and consumer shifts toward sustainability.

Similarly, companies with strong social and governance practices tend to have more engaged employees, increased productivity, purposeful teams, stronger brand loyalty, and lower operational risks due to a minor risk of contingencies in general, both technical and labor. The emphasis on governance and ethical leadership helps businesses navigate challenges more effectively.

Talking about regulatory changes on the sight, governments and their monitoring bodies worldwide are implementing or considering regulations that mandate ESG reporting and disclosure. For example, the European Union (EU) has introduced the Sustainable Finance Disclosure Regulation (SFDR)—which aims to improve the clarity and comparability of sustainability disclosures in financial market participants' investment policies and products and the Corporate Sustainability Reporting Directive (CSRD), which make businesses more publicly accountable by obliging them to regularly disclose information on their societal and environmental impact. So, CSRD requires companies to report on a broad range of sustainability issues, not just climate-related risks.

Also, more and more corporations commit publicly to reaching sustainability targets by announcing that the organization will be net zero by a specific date. In this sense, Forbes Magazine in a May 2024 article explained that:[7]

7. Forbes 2024 Net-Zero Leaders List—Top Eco-Friendly Companies, https://www.forbes.com/lists/net-zero-leaders/.

> Sustainability commitments are booming. The number of companies working on significant environmental pledges with the Science Based Targets Initiative (a global project of nonprofits including the United Nations Global Compact) rose from 2,079 in 2022 to 4,204 by the end of 2023.

Corporate net-zero pledges have multiplied in recent years, and they include pledges made by countries, companies, and other organizations to reduce their GHG emissions to net zero by a specified date, often by 2050. Achieving net zero means that any remaining GHG emissions are balanced by removing an equivalent amount from the atmosphere. These commitments comprise:

(1) Emission Reductions:
- Scope 1: Direct emissions from owned or controlled sources.
- Scope 2: Indirect emissions from the generation of purchased electricity, steam, heating, and cooling consumed by the reporting entity.
- Scope 3: All other indirect emissions that occur in a company's value chain, including both upstream and downstream emissions.

(2) Carbon Removal:
- Methods to remove carbon from the atmosphere, such as reforestation, soil carbon sequestration, and direct air capture technologies.

Numerous companies across various industries have set net-zero targets. For instance, Microsoft aims to be carbon-negative by 2030,[8] Unilever has committed to net-zero emissions across its value chain by 2039,[9] and Telefonica aims to achieve net-zero emissions by 2040.[10]

Also, many countries have committed to net-zero targets, often as part of their Nationally Determined Contributions (NDCs) under the Paris Agreement. For example, the EU aims to be climate-neutral by 2050, and China has pledged to achieve carbon neutrality by 2060.

As an impressive example of this historical shift, the EU wind and solar power reached new highs in the first half of 2024, reaching a 30 % share of the bloc's electricity generation and overtaking fossil fuels for the first time, according to a report from climate think-tank Ember,[11] that says:

> The first half of 2024 shows the EU's electricity transition in full swing, as wind and solar grew fast enough to outpace demand growth and push fossil fuels out of the mix. The EU's swift action to reduce dependency on fossil fuels was evident as new wind and solar capacity came online, marking a permanent structural change.

---

8. Our Sustainability Journey | Microsoft CSR, https://www.microsoft.com/en-us/corporate-responsibility/sustainability-journey?msockid=09f2e3af7bee699b15a8f7e17a7e68ff.
9. Addressing climate change with action | Unilever, https://www.unilever.com/sustainability/climate/.
10. Telefónica moves towards net zero by 2040 through energy efficiency—Telefónica (telefonica.com), https://www.telefonica.com/en/communication-room/press-room/telefonica-moves-towards-net-zero-by-2040-through-energy-efficiency/.
11. Available at: Wind and solar overtake EU fossil fuels in the first half of 2024 | Ember (ember-climate.org), https://ember-climate.org/insights/research/eu-wind-and-solar-overtake-fossil-fuels/#supporting-material.

Net-zero commitments are crucial in the global effort to mitigate climate change and limit global warming. While the path to achieving these commitments is complex and ambitious, they represent a critical step towards a sustainable and resilient future.

Consequently, this is a reality for the mergers and acquisitions (M&A) market, which is significantly influenced by net-zero commitments in several ways. And some poor results on ESG due diligence efforts led to several deal breakers for potential M&A operations. According to a 2023 study made by KPMG:[12]

> A survey carried out by KPMG US has shown that 66% of survey participants from the Europe, the Middle East and Africa (EMA) region said that material findings from Environmental, Social and Governance Due Diligence (ESG-DD) had led to cancellations of deals, while 62% said that they had resulted in reductions in the purchasing price.
>
> These statistics emphasize the significant value which ESG due diligence can bring, and the risks of not doing it. Carrying out ESG DD makes the dealmaker far better informed as to the potential ESG risks and benefits of a planned transaction.
>
> A well-developed and defined ESG (Environmental, Social and Governance) strategy is increasingly becoming a pre-requisite for a successful business and is no longer merely a "nice to have." Regulation on ESG issues is strengthening in many parts of the world, and so is media attention to cases of noncompliance with ESG principles. Today, a company's clients, employees and other stakeholders are much more likely to expect it to have strong ESG policies.

All this buzz about the integration of dealmaking and ESG has a lot to do with legit concerns about environmental topics and net-zero commitments but also with the reality of corporate reputation and stakeholders' (consumers, investors, employees, and the public) expectations. Companies are increasingly expected to act ethically and responsibly in their environmental, social, and governance practices.

Also, most large companies worldwide are more and more investing in sustainability-related opportunities; in accordance with a recently launched survey presented by Deloitte,[13] "climate change remains a top three issue for global C-suite level business leaders (CxOs), surpassing political uncertainty, competition for talent, and the changing regulatory environment, among others. A key indicator of climate's staying power on leaders' agendas is that 85% of CxOs say they have increased investments in sustainability in the past year—up from 75% in 2023—and half have started to implement technology solutions to help achieve climate goals."

Nivea's (worldwide recognized by its blue can cream) example is also clarifying, as the company demonstrates its concerns with sustainability by stating that:

> The fight against climate change is humankind's most important environmental challenge. That is why NIVEA's vision is about taking climate care and we have set ambitious climate targets on a company level that are in line with the latest climate

12. Over Half of M&A Dealmakers Have Cancelled Deals on ESG Due Diligence Findings: KPMG Survey—ESG Today, https://www.esgtoday.com/over-half-of-ma-dealmakers-have-cancelled-deals-on-esg-due-diligence-findings-kpmg-survey/.
13. Executives say sustainability investments are up, new Deloitte research reveals | Deloitte Global, https://www.deloitte.com/global/en/about/press-room/executives-say-sustainability-investments-are-up-new-deloitte-research-reveals.html.

> science. These targets not only cover the significant reduction of CO_2 emissions at our production sites, but also extend to the indirect emissions associated with our overall value chain such as the ingredients and packaging materials we use for our NIVEA products.

This is an authentic and legitimate concern, and it is especially important when social media plays a crucial role in both ESG and cancel culture, as it amplifies public scrutiny and can rapidly mobilize collective action against companies perceived to be acting unethically or irresponsibly, whose consequence can be boycotts, protests, and negative publicity.

A strong ESG performance can somehow shield and boost a company's brand reputation. Conversely, ignoring ESG issues can lead to reputational damage, which is often exacerbated by cancel culture. Companies that are perceived as not taking their ESG responsibilities seriously can quickly become targets for public criticism, mainly if they fail on ethical standards, such as labor practices, human rights, and community engagement.

c ETHICAL SUPPLY CHAIN

Cancel culture, amplified by social media, can significantly harm a company's reputation and even threaten its survival. This extends beyond a company's practices to its entire supply chain.

So, aiming to reduce this risk, it is fundamental to ensure its suppliers are oriented by socially responsible and environmentally sustainable commitments.

It comprises ethical practices in the procurement, production, and distribution of products and includes the knowledge that all workers receive fair wages and work in safe and human conditions under compliance with local labor laws and international standards, such as those set by the International Labor Organization (ILO), as for example, the prohibition of the use of child labor or forced labor at any stage of the supply chain.

According to the ILO, forced labor refers to any work or service performed under coercion or the threat of penalty, without the worker's voluntary consent.

From an environmental standpoint, it includes using resources efficiently to minimize waste (through reduction, reuse, and recycling) and minimizing environmental impact by adopting practices that conserve water, energy, and raw materials. Also, it is relevant to take steps to reduce GHG emissions across the supply chain, from sourcing raw materials to product delivery.

Identifying potential risks in the supply chain related to labor practices, environmental impact, ethical sourcing, and implementing strategies to mitigate these risks. Note that sometimes businesses have limited visibility into or control over suppliers, especially the links located in emerging markets.

Meanwhile, the stakeholders are demanding greater accountability from companies, who are under pressure to take responsibility for the impact of their operations and to ensure that they're doing business in an ethical, sustainable, and fair fashion:

companies can become sustainable solely by teaming up with suppliers to follow ESG principles.

Until now, the decision to resolve ESG issues in supply chains has rested mainly on reputational risks, and it may lead to a decrease in revenues, lower profits, a hindered access to capital, declining valuations and attractiveness as employers.

However, some regulations are being released about this topic: the broadest of these initiatives is the EU's Corporate Sustainability Due Diligence Directive (CSDDD), which was ratified by the European Commission in 2022 and adopted by the EU Parliament in April 2024. According to this regulation, companies must identify, prevent, mitigate, and account for human rights and environmental impacts throughout their supply chains, and it encompasses their own operations, their subsidiaries, and their value chain (both upstream and downstream).

It requires both EU and non-EU companies operating in the EU to take responsibility for the environmental and social impacts of their value chains, including those of suppliers and their sub-suppliers and business partners, imposing substantial fines (of as much as 5% of global turnover), in case abuses are identified. It aims to foster sustainable and responsible corporate behavior throughout global supply chains, promote liable corporate behavior, protect human rights, and boost environmental sustainability.

As an immediate consequence of CSDDD, companies must conduct thorough due diligence processes to identify potential risks and address them appropriately, and they may face legal consequences for failing to comply with the directive, including potential civil liability for harm caused by their failure to exercise adequate due diligence. Corporate boards and executives will have direct responsibility for ensuring compliance with due diligence requirements.

Similarly, the EU Deforestation Regulation aims to combat global deforestation and forest degradation operated by the EU's demand for certain commodities. The regulation demands companies to place specific products on the EU market to ensure that these products are "deforestation-free" and that they have not contributed to deforestation or forest degradation after a specific cutoff date.

So, the purpose of this legislation is to promote sustainable supply chains by ensuring that commodities entering the EU market are sourced responsibly and are not linked to deforestation. This involves requiring companies to exercise due diligence, trace the origin of the commodities, and ensure compliance with the regulation's standards.

According to the Delegation of the EU to Ghana,[14] the country—which exported 62% of the cocoa it produced to the EU in 2022—started to use a system that traces cocoa beans from farm to port. And this is a direct reflection of the new regulation that demands the EU importers of coffee, cocoa, soy, palm, timber, beef and rubber to demonstrate their supply chains are not causing deforestation anywhere in the world.

On the other side of the ocean, the U.S. government issued Executive Order 14,017 ("America's Supply Chains Act"), defining a complete review of critical supply

14. Unpacking the EU Deforestation Regulation for Ghana's cocoa industry | EEAS (europa.eu), https://www.eeas.europa.eu/delegations/ghana/unpacking-eu-deforestation-regulation-ghana%E2%80%99s-cocoa-industry_en?s=101.

chains to address vulnerabilities and promote resilience. It focuses on sectors such as pharmaceuticals, semiconductors, and critical minerals.

The focus is slightly different from the European one, as it is more concentrated on addressing vulnerabilities in the supply chains of essential goods, services, and critical sectors, thus making the U.S. better prepared to respond to crises and reduce dependency on foreign supply chains, enhancing national security and economic stability.

Note that California state has a specific regulation about ethics in the supply chain, the California Transparency in Supply Chains Act. This law requires large companies doing business in California to disclose their efforts to reject human trafficking and slavery from their direct supply chains. Companies must report their verification, audits, certifications, internal accountability, and training related to human trafficking and slavery.

In any case, U.S. consumers in general are aware of responsible corporate behavior in the supply chains. To illustrate it, it is relevant to bring the words of Senior Vice President of supply chain applications at Oracle, Jon Chorley:[15]

> It is clear that most U.S. consumers—and businesses wanting to sell to those consumers—want to ensure that goods and services are sourced ethically and sustainably.
>
> A growing segment of consumers have become educated and engaged on Environmental, Social, and Governance (ESG) initiatives and are letting their activism guide their purchasing behavior. According to one recent study, 93 percent of consumers surveyed believe that social and environmental issues are more critical than ever, and 88 percent now consider the sustainability impact of both the business and its partners (i.e. its supply chain) before buying from it.
>
> And yet, despite this growing sentiment, most businesses still only have visibility into their tier one suppliers. Their longer-distance view into their suppliers' suppliers tends to be hazy at best.
>
> Gaining a better look into tier one, tier two, and tier three suppliers (suppliers of their suppliers' suppliers) can be incredibly complex, but for U.S. companies, it's now a legal requirement. Shipments of goods from certain regions into U.S. ports can now be stopped due to concerns about how the products were manufactured, with what materials, and by whom.

Likewise, a recent (and positive) example of a financing supply chain aiming to avoid compliance issues is the announcement made in August 2024 by Citibank and the World Bank Group's International Finance Corporation (IFC) about the creation of a new USD 2 billion emerging markets sustainable supply chain finance program to suppliers dealing with transactions both with domestic and international buyers.[16]

15. Building Ethical Supply Chains (forbes.com), https://www.forbes.com/sites/jonchorley/2022/08/31/building-ethical-supply-chains/.
16. Citi, IFC Launch $2 Billion Sustainable Supply Chain Finance Program—The Financial Analyst, https://thefinancialanalyst.net/2024/08/06/citi-ifc-launch-2-billion-sustainable-supply-chain-finance-program/#:~:text=Citi%20and%20the%20World%20Bank%20Group%E2%80%99s%20International%20Finance,%28GSCF%29%20and%20represents%20its%20largest%20project%20to%20date.

Surely, these financial institutions are aware that an ethical supply chain is one that prioritizes fair labor practices, environmental sustainability, strong corporate governance, and effective risk management, and it needs financing to be made available to small- and medium-sized enterprises (SMEs).

This holistic approach not only helps with building a responsible business but also contributes to long-term success and sustainability, as well as minimizes risks from being canceled.

d CLIMATE CHANGE AND THE TASK FORCE ON CLIMATE-RELATED FINANCIAL DISCLOSURES

As Earth's climate changes, extreme weather events are happening across the planet: record-breaking heat waves, drenching rains, severe inundations, years-long droughts, extreme wildfires, and hurricanes leading to widespread floodings, and depletion of water supply are all becoming more habitual and intense.

Physical risks from these weather events add new considerations for assets in view of the threat of significant damage and associated disruption to corporate operations and supply chains.

As the environmental world is intensely interconnected with the social, macro-economic and political world, the impacts of the climate crisis will trigger a broader chain of cascading effects on ecosystems, agricultural yields, and human health, which will then have ramifications on our lives and livelihoods.

This is a deep new challenge we are facing worldwide: the inability to duly predict extreme climate events that seemingly come out of nowhere and wreak devastation and are becoming more usual due to warming temperatures.

The social consequences of climate change will affect the poorest economies more, where a large part of the population depends directly on activities that may be the most impacted by this phenomenon, mainly the agricultural, forestry, and fisheries sectors, since low-income people are the most likely to depend for their survival on resources provided by nature.

Also, rising temperatures are worsening disparities in access to clean water and affordable food. Frequently, the poorest populations do not access insurance mechanisms or have basic health services, making them most vulnerable to any shock reaching their assets and income streams.

A striking example is Jakarta, Indonesia, which is sinking due to rising sea levels from the surrounding Java Sea. Illegal wells dug for clean water exacerbate the issue, forcing the capital to be relocated. Today, 40% of Jakarta (a city whose population is 11 million people) lies below sea level, and flooding is increasingly common. Jakarta is sinking. Then, Indonesia's president, Joko Widodo, thought of a solution: he is moving the country's capital, about 800 miles from the current one.

Another illustrative case of how companies are reacting to climate change is Google, which uses AI for forecasting through investment in technologies that can support communities in getting prepared for natural disasters and answering climate-related disasters and their threats.[17]

> To build effective AI solutions, researchers need a solid understanding of the challenges faced by people around the world. This includes getting access to data that's representative of the problems, partnering with domain experts to make sure we're building reliable systems, following policy guidance on regulatory structures, and finding real-world opportunities for testing these systems. For these reasons, collaboration with affected communities, scientists, industry professionals, regulators, and governments is central to our sustainability efforts.
>
> If you are an industry domain expert or climate scientist with a specific challenge to solve that could help the world understand, mitigate, or adapt to climate change, our climate & sustainability team would love to hear from you.

This paragraph above is an example of how these new issues may generate job opportunities for the ones who are dedicated to preparing themselves for the green agenda requirements, as mentioned at the end of Chapter 1.

In any case, climate change is a global challenge. No matter your industry, location, or role, its effects impact the way we live and work. Coping with it from a risk management perspective involves identifying, assessing, and mitigating the various risks associated. This approach includes:

- Identification: (i) to detect direct impacts like the consequences of sea level rise and the effects of sudden temperature changes; and (ii) to quantify the shift towards a low-carbon economy, such as strategy changes, technological shifts, and market changes.
- Assessment: by determining which assets, regions, and communities are most vulnerable to climate impacts and developing and analyzing different scenarios to understand potential future liabilities by using data and models to estimate the probability and potential costs of climate-related risks to reduce the exposure to potential legal claims due to failure to mitigate or adapt to climate change.
- Mitigation: to implement measures to reduce GHG emissions, such as transition to cleaner energy sources, energy efficiency and carbon offsetting.

By taking a comprehensive and proactive approach, organizations can effectively manage the risks associated with climate change and enhance their resilience to its impacts. To do so, the Task Force on Climate-Related Financial Disclosures (TCFD) is the initial platform that provides information to investors about what companies are doing to reduce the risks of climate change, as well as being transparent about the way in which they are governed.

TCFD was established in December 2015 by the Group of 20 (an intergovernmental forum comprising 19 Ministers of Finances from sovereign countries, the EU, and

17. Using AI to fight climate change—Google DeepMind, https://deepmind.google/discover/blog/using-ai-to-fight-climate-change/.

the African Union), and it is chaired by Michael Bloomberg, who served as the mayor of New York City for three terms from 2002 to 2013.

TCFD aims to improve and increase the reporting of climate-related financial information and to help stakeholders better understand the financial implications of climate change through the development of consistent climate-related financial risk disclosures.

Its guidelines are applicable to corporations across all sectors and jurisdictions. While initially aimed at large, publicly listed companies, its parameters can be adopted by any company looking to improve the way they assess and disclose climate-related risk.

The International Sustainability Standards Board (ISSB)[18] recently published its inaugural standards, IFRS S1 and IFRS S2, which fully incorporate the TCFD recommendations. These standards determine a global baseline for sustainability-related disclosures, aiming that companies worldwide will follow consistent and unified guidelines in reporting climate-related information.

Note climate change-related risks and opportunities may influence an entity's cash flows (due to increased costs for energy, raw materials, and insurance because of more frequent and severe weather events, as well as causing asset impairments) and access to finance or cost of capital through current and anticipated effects (due to the growing availability of green financing options for companies that demonstrate strong sustainability practices, stating that these funds can provide more favorable terms compared to traditional financing).

Although originally shaped as a voluntary framework, many jurisdictions are now incorporating these regulations into official guidelines or legislations. Therefore, voluntary sustainability reporting gives way to mandatory reporting, as climate reporting is in the spotlights, providing more visibility into company's actions, plans, risks and opportunities related to this challenge.

e SUSTAINABLE FINANCE

Sustainability has become a key focus in recent years, driven largely by the transition to a low-carbon economy and the global awareness of climate change. Green talks are everywhere—in political debates, corporate boardrooms, and in family and friends' chats. It is happening because sustainability matters, and it is crucial now, since the effects of climate change have become more evident and society's call for action has spread louder.

This new outlook also led to a change in investors' mindset: they traditionally evaluated the performance of their investments solely based on financial measures, such as return on investment, i.e., to evaluate the efficiency or profitability of an investment.

18. In November 2021, the International Financial Reporting Standards (IFRS) Foundation announced that it would form the International Sustainability Standards Board (ISSB) to develop centralized standards for climate disclosure reporting.

However, investing with an eye to environmental or social issues, not just its efficiency or profitability, has become mainstream. Or, as published by the World Economic Forum in a 2022 analysis,[19] introducing people to this topic:

> The drive to sustainability is transforming the way we live. But what is the impact on the way our savings and pensions are invested? Welcome to the world of sustainable finance.
>
> Environmental, social and governance (ESG) considerations have come to dominate many investment decisions in recent years. Put simply, this means investing your money where it will make the world a better place.

Therefore, sustainable finance means a huge move in how financial services can sponsor a more equitable and more sustainable future. This belief highlights the need to support economic growth while reducing pressures on the environment, focusing on social inequities, and aiming for long-term sustainability.

Sustainable finance is not simply an ethical choice; it is a pragmatic answer to the global claims presented by social disparities, climate change and natural resource depletion.

It comprises a broad range of activities, including sustainability-linked bonds, green bonds, social impact investing, ESG-focused asset management, and climate financing. All of them are designed to fund projects and businesses that have a positive impact on the environment and society, such as energy transition to net zero, sustainable agriculture, affordable housing, and accessible healthcare. So, it is important for several reasons:

(1) Mitigating Climate Change: By financing capital to projects that reduce GHG emissions and contribute to energy efficiency, sustainable finance plays a critical role in addressing climate change and supporting a low-carbon economy.
(2) Preserving Natural Resources: Sustainable finance encourages investments in flood mitigation, sustainable agriculture, and resource-efficient technologies, helping to preserve natural resources for future generations.
(3) Reducing Risks: ESG factors can be material to financial performance, as the adequate management of ESG risks is often better positioned to avoid regulatory penalties, reputational damage, and operational liabilities. Companies that prioritize sustainability can enhance their reputation and build trust with consumers, investors, and other stakeholders, leading to stronger brand loyalty and competitive advantage.
(4) Meeting Investor Demand: There is a growing demand from investors, especially younger generations, for investment opportunities that align with their values. Sustainable finance provides options for investors to support positive environmental and social outcomes while seeking financial returns.

19. What is sustainable finance & how it is changing the world | World Economic Forum (weforum.org), https://www.weforum.org/agenda/2022/01/what-is-sustainable-finance/.

(5) Boosting Social Equity: Investments that prioritize social criteria can enhance living conditions, health, and education in underserved communities, contributing to greater social equity and inclusion.

As it is in the interest of governments to attract investment in green bonds, some tax benefits are associated with them. In France, for example, tax relief is offered for investments in sustainable development funds, which are designated as "Plan d'Épargne en Actions" and focus on environmentally and socially responsible companies.

Of course, it varies by jurisdiction and can significantly enhance their attractiveness to investors and issuers. These incentives help channel investment into environmentally sustainable projects, aligning financial markets with broader climate and sustainability goals.

So, green bonds are usually directed to fund green projects, i.e., projects that are sustainable and socially responsible in areas as diverse as energy efficiency, clean energy and transportation, circular economy or responsible waste management. As explained by the United States Environmental Protection Agency,[20] when describing these types of bonds:

> Green bonds are a bond instrument that use proceeds to finance or refinance environmental, water, or clean energy projects. Green bonds are attractive financing tools as they couple financial returns and environmental benefits (e.g., improved air quality, reduced water use), do not require any new legislation, and are typically tax-exempt. Green bonds help governments finance new projects while enabling investors to reach sustainability targets. Investors include, but are not limited to, institutional investors such as insurance companies or pension funds.
>
> Green bonds have similar risk-return profiles as municipal bonds; however, the green bonds framework, which specifies the green alignment of the bonds, may require providing more transparency into their environmental, social, and governance (ESG) risks relative to other municipal bonds from the same municipal issuer. The attractiveness of a bond to investors depends, in part, on the credit rating of the issuing body. Green bonds are also an effective way for policymakers to signal energy efficiency and renewable energy policy priorities.

Countries can release green bonds aiming to raise money for their projects. For instance, the Brazilian Federal government launched its Sovereign Sustainable Bond Framework in 2023 to support sustainable development. As explained by the World Bank:[21]

> With $7.2 billion of sustainable debt issued in 2022, Brazil ranked first regionally for corporate green bonds, having raised money for climate and biodiversity projects. On September 5, 2023, the Federal government, in its effort to support

20. Municipal Bonds and Green Bonds | U.S. EPA, https://www.epa.gov/statelocalenergy/municipal-bonds-and-green-bonds.
21. Brazil Sovereign Sustainable Bond: Financing a greener, more inclusive, and equitable economy (worldbank.org), https://www.worldbank.org/en/news/feature/2024/02/08/brazil-sovereign-sustainable-bond-financing-a-greener-more-inclusive-and-equitable-economy.

sustainable development, launched its Sovereign Sustainable Bond Framework. A reference document that enables the country to issue green, social, and sustainability bonds to finance budgetary programs with positive environmental and/or social impacts.

Another interesting example comes from the giant Spanish energy company, Iberdrola, which raised a USD 525 million green bond, aiming to invest in its network and renewable energy in the U.S.[22]

Going beyond, there are some companies whose objective is primarily to invest in sustainability. Breakthrough Energy, the climate-focused initiative set up by Microsoft co-founder Bill Gates, is a good example. It was launched in 2015 to invest in technologies that may solve problems associated with climate change and other clean tech initiatives.

This giant investment coalition includes more than two dozen industry leaders, including Bill Gates, Amazon's Jeff Bezos, Salesforce CEO Marc Benioff, Meta's Mark Zuckerberg and Alibaba CEO Jack Ma.

In a post on his Gates Notes blog, Gates said this fund will invest more than USD 1 billion in scientific discoveries able to provide cheap and reliable clean energy to the world:

> By the middle of this century, the world will use twice as much energy as we use today.
>
> There's good news in this: more energy means better lives and stronger economies.
>
> But it also means the world needs a new energy supply—one that doesn't contribute to climate change. Climate change is a serious threat, especially in the poorest parts of the world.
>
> We need affordable and reliable energy that doesn't emit greenhouse gas to power the future—and to get it, we need a different model for investing in good ideas and moving them from the lab to the market.

And, as defined on the Breakthrough Energy website:[23]

> Humans have been innovating in all these areas for thousands of years—but energy transitions can take centuries, and we don't have time to wait. Right now, we need the most ambitious innovation program the world has ever seen to build and scale clean technologies that can compete with the ones we're using now.
>
> At Breakthrough Energy, we are committed to supporting new technologies that change the way we live, eat, work, travel, and make things so we can avoid the most devastating impacts of climate change. We believe that funding cutting-edge research; investing in new clean technologies as they evolve from idea to commercial adoption; crafting smart, tailored, and scalable energy policies; and

22. Iberdrola places USD 525 million in 10-year green bonds in the U.S. with strong investor demand—Iberdrola, https://www.iberdrola.com/press-room/news/detail/iberdrola-places-usd-525-million-in-10-year-green-bonds-in-the-us-with-strong-investor-demand#: ~ :text = New %20successful%20financing%20operation%20for%20Iberdrola.%20Iberdrola%2C%20through,US%20for%20USD%20525%20million%20%28EUR%20490%20million%29.
23. Our Approach | Breakthrough Energy, https://www.breakthroughenergy.org/our-approach/.

forging deep partnerships among policymakers, innovators, and industry leaders will lead to positive solutions that can bring clean energy to all.

Recently, the company raised USD 839 million for its third venture capital fund,[24] Breakthrough Energy Ventures III. This fund invests in startups that offer solutions for the production, storage, and distribution of energy in a sustainable way, as well as innovations capable of reducing GHG emissions throughout the global economy, leading to the development of sustainable products and services.

A myriad of other examples can be mentioned, from corporations investing in initiatives that need huge financing to scale, such as decarbonization, sustainability innovations and infrastructure to protect vulnerable communities. And some of this investment has some tax benefits, such as tax exemptions and tax credits to bondholders instead of traditional interest payments.

However, the fact is: all these brilliant minds working together in the same entrepreneurial idea confirm the idea that a massive inflow of funds is being directed to sustainable economic growth. It empowers investors, corporations, and individuals to associate their financial activities with wider societal goals.

And this is the biggest business opportunity for our generation.

f UNITED NATION'S SUSTAINABLE DEVELOPMENT GOALS

When talking about wider societal goals, it is binding to consider Sustainable Development Goals (SDGs), also known as the Global Goals, adopted by the United Nations in 2015 as a widespread demand for action to end poverty, protect the planet, and ensure that by 2030 all people enjoy peace and prosperity.

These 17 goals—mentioned below—are connected and manifest desirable societal goals towards a better world:[25]

(1) Poverty Eradication
(2) Zero Hunger
(3) Good Health and Well-Being
(4) Quality Education
(5) Gender Equality
(6) Clean Water and Sanitation
(7) Affordable and Clean Energy
(8) Decent Work and Economic Growth
(9) Industry, Innovation, and Infrastructure
(10) Reduced Inequalities
(11) Sustainable Cities and Communities
(12) Responsible Consumption and Production
(13) Climate Action

24. Bill Gates' Breakthrough Energy is raising another big fund for clean energy and climate investing—GeekWire, https://www.geekwire.com/2024/bill-gates-breakthrough-energy-is-raising-another-big-fund-for-clean-energy-and-climate-investing/.
25. THE 17 GOALS | Sustainable Development (un.org), https://sdgs.un.org/goals.

(14) Life Below Water
(15) Life on Land
(16) Peace, Justice, and Strong Institutions
(17) Partnerships for the Goals.

These SDGs act as a roadmap for governments, businesses, and civil society to work together towards common objectives, ensuring that development is sustainable, inclusive, and equitable.

However, the progress toward achieving the SDGs by the target year 2030 is not fully achievable. Indeed, there were some significant advancements in some areas; on the other hand, considerable challenges in others, mainly connected to the lingering effects of the pandemics.

Roughly speaking, this is the current panorama for each of the SDGs, as updated by the United Nation's website:[26]

(1) No Poverty (SDG 1):
- **Progress**: The global poverty rate has been declining, but the COVID-19 pandemic reversed some gains, pushing millions back into extreme poverty.
- **Challenges**: Economic shocks, conflicts, and climate change continue to impede progress.

(2) Zero Hunger (SDG 2):
- **Progress**: Agricultural productivity was transformed *with new technologies and applications* and food security has improved in some regions.
- **Challenges**: Hunger and food insecurity have been intensified by conflicts, climate change, and economic downturns, with millions still facing severe food deficiencies.

(3) Good Health and Well-Being (SDG 3):
- **Progress**: Life expectancy has increased, and significant strides have been made in reducing child mortality. Education is widespread, homicide rates are dropping and diseases are increasingly curable, battling diseases like HIV/AIDS, malaria, and tuberculosis.
- **Challenges**: The pandemic damaged healthcare systems and slowed progress on many health indicators. Also, well-being is threatened by the amplified use of social media and its side effects (e.g., comparison, sense of anxiety and fake news).

(4) Quality Education (SDG 4):
- **Progress**: Access to education has increased, with notable progress in early childhood education.

26. The-Sustainable-Development-Goals-Report-2024.pdf (un.org), https://unstats.un.org/sdgs/report/2024/The-Sustainable-Development-Goals-Report-2024.pdf.

- **Challenges**: Disparities in education quality and access remain, especially for marginalized groups, and the pandemic has led to relevant learning losses.

(5) Gender Equality (SDG 5):
- **Progress**: There has been progress in reducing gender disparities in education, political representation, and labor force participation.
- **Challenges**: Gender-based violence, salary gaps, and underrepresentation in leadership persist.

(6) Clean Water and Sanitation (SDG 6):
- **Progress**: Access to clean drinking water and sanitation has improved and policies for the adequate reuse of the resource have been established.
- **Challenges**: Many regions still lack consistent access to these essential services, and water scarcity is becoming more critical due to climate change and over-extraction.

(7) Affordable and Clean Energy (SDG 7):
- **Progress**: Renewable energy capacity has grown, and more people have access to electricity.
- **Challenges**: There is still a need for greater investment in sustainable energy infrastructure, especially in least-developed countries.

(8) Decent Work and Economic Growth (SDG 8):
- **Progress**: Many countries have seen economic growth and job creation, some of which are connected to new technologies and innovation on sustainability.
- **Challenges**: Economic inequalities persist, and the pandemic caused significant job losses and economic setbacks.

(9) Industry, Innovation, and Infrastructure (SDG 9):
- **Progress**: Infrastructure development and innovation are advancing in many regions. Increased investment in research and development.
- **Challenges**: Investment gaps in infrastructure and technology remain, particularly in low-income countries.

(10) Reduced Inequality (SDG 10):
- **Progress**: Some progress in reducing income inequality within countries. It was punctual and more connected to more education opportunities.
- **Challenges**: Inequality between countries and among different social groups is still high, exacerbated by the pandemic. Wealth inequality is a real challenge.

(11) Sustainable Cities and Communities (SDG 11):
- **Progress**: Efforts to create sustainable urban environments are underway.
- **Challenges**: Rapid urbanization, ineffective infrastructure, and environmental degradation pose significant obstacles.

(12) Responsible Consumption and Production (SDG 12):
- **Progress**: Awareness and initiatives around conscious and sustainable consumption are growing.
- **Challenges**: Overconsumption and waste management issues remain critical problems.

(13) Climate Action (SDG 13):
- **Progress**: Global sensitivity, awareness and commitments to combat climate change are increasing.
- **Challenges**: GHG emissions are still rising, and climate change impacts are becoming more severe.

(14) Life Below Water (SDG 14):
- **Progress**: Efforts to protect marine ecosystems are gaining traction.
- **Challenges**: Sea pollution and climate change continue to threaten marine life.

(15) Life on Land (SDG 15):
- **Progress**: Conservation efforts and reforestation projects are expanding. The sale of carbon credits is gaining momentum.
- **Challenges**: Deforestation, habitat loss, and biodiversity decline are still major issues.

(16) Peace, Justice, and Strong Institutions (SDG 16):
- **Progress**: Some regions have seen improvements in governance and reductions in violence.
- **Challenges**: Conflicts, dictatorships, corruption, and weak institutions remain widespread.

(17) Partnerships for the Goals (SDG 17):
- **Progress**: Global partnerships and cooperation have strengthened.
- **Challenges**: Financial and technical support for achieving the SDGs is deficient, and international cooperation needs to be enhanced.

Overall, while there has been expressive progress toward many of the SDGs, significant challenges and setbacks, particularly due to all the harm triggered by the COVID-19 pandemic and ongoing conflicts, mean that much work remains to be done to achieve these ambitious goals by 2030. Increased global assistance, investment, and innovation are essential to accelerating progress and reducing inequalities in the remaining years.

And another powerful tool to keep progressing in the SDGs is the adoption of an effective and equitable tax system. By mobilizing resources, promoting fairness, boosting research and development and incentivizing sustainable practices, taxation can significantly contribute to the achievement of a more prosperous, equitable, and sustainable world.

As indicated earlier, taxation is the key theme of this book, and this will be the next chapters' core discussion topics.

CHAPTER 3
Purpose of Taxation

a ROSETTA STONE AND A QUICK HISTORY OF TAXATION

Until the 19th century, the study of ancient Egypt relied on limited sources and interpretations because most of the ancient Egyptians' written records, inscribed in hieroglyphics, were unreadable.

So, to study this civilization—known for its extensive contributions to various aspects of human civilization, from art and architecture to science, religion, and governance—scholars relied on classical Greek literature about Egypt, and these sources were often secondhand and contained inaccuracies, myths, and misconceptions.

However, in 1799, French engineers doing demolition work in the Egyptian delta town of El-Rashid (renamed as "Rosetta") made a highly significant discovery: while pulling down a wall, they uncovered a large black granite stone with parallel inscriptions in two languages (Greek and Egyptian). This stone (named "Rosetta Stone") was crucial to the decoding of Egyptian hieroglyphics, and it was deciphered by the French scholar Jean-François Champollion.

Today, the Rosetta Stone is one of the world's best-known archaeological relics, seen by millions of visitors at the British Museum every year.

But what does the text on the stone say?

It records a series of concessions awarded by the king to the clergy in 196 BCE, including tax exemptions and other privileges, as a reward for their support to the king. This aspect of the text reveals the administrative and economic considerations of the Ptolemaic dynasty, highlighting the role of taxation in maintaining loyalty and control.

Therefore, the Rosetta Stone, our key to unlocking the meaning of hieroglyphics and understanding deeply Egyptian civilization, was basically a tax document.

Besides this fantastic story, the History of taxation has some other highlights, all of them reflecting the development of governance, social structures, and economic systems from ancient times to the modern era. This fascinating journey through the evolution of societies and economies has some major milestones:

(1) Ancient Civilizations:
- Mesopotamia (circa 3000 BCE): One of the first recorded systems of taxation was in Mesopotamia, where citizens paid taxes in the form of livestock, grain, or labor. Farmers were required to pay taxes in the form of a portion of their crops. Commonly taxed crops included barley, wheat, dates, and other agricultural products. If not possible to pay taxes on goods, citizens often provided labor for public works and state projects, such as building canals, temples, and city walls. This system, known as "corvée labor," was a system where citizens were required to perform unpaid labor for the state.
- Ancient Egypt (circa 2800 BCE): The taxation system was highly centralized, with the pharaoh exercising ultimate authority over tax collection and administration. Local officials, known as Nomarchs, were responsible for collecting taxes in their regions and reporting to the central government. Taxes were charged on agricultural produce, which were collected by scribes and used to fund state projects, including the construction of pyramids. The temples were major economic entities, owning vast pieces of land and employing many people. Taxes collected from these lands and activities contributed to the state's wealth. So, the text mentioned in the Rosetta Stone is adequate to the whole context, since it is about a tax exemption granted to the clergy.
- Ancient Greece (circa 600 BCE): Taxes varied significantly between city-states, with Athens and Sparta being the most notable examples. In general, it was levied on property and income to fund public projects, military expenses, and religious festivals. It was quite complex, as it also included custom duties, harbor taxes and "liturgies," i.e., the requirement for wealthy citizens to finance public services voluntarily. Also, "eisphora" (a type of war tax) was charged.

(2) Roman Empire (circa 500 BCE-476 CE):
- The Romans implemented various taxes, including an individual tax, generally imposed on free non-citizens and slaves within the Roman provinces, charged through a fixed amount per person, regardless of income or wealth. Also, a land tax was charged based on the ownership and productivity of land. Taxes were used to fund the military, infrastructure, and public services.

(3) Medieval Europe (5th-15th Century):
- Feudal System: Taxes were primarily in the form of feudal dues and obligations, as serfs and peasants were required to provide labor for their lords on a regular basis, similar to "corvée labor" which included working on the lord's land, repairing roads, or building structures. Peasants paid taxes to their lords, who in turn owed military service and

taxes to the king. Also, serfs owed various dues in kind, such as a portion of their agricultural produce, livestock, or other goods.
- Church Taxes: The Catholic Church collected tithes, a religious tax which was mandatory was paid amounting to one-tenth of an individual's income.

(4) Early Modern Period (16th-18th Century):
- Mercantilism: European nations used taxes and tariffs to promote domestic industries, and it was closely aligned with the economic goals of maximizing state wealth and power. It involved a range of taxes designed to protect and promote domestic industries, control trade, and support government expenditures, particularly for military and colonial purposes. The mercantilist approach to taxation laid the groundwork for later economic policies and fiscal practices. Colonies were taxed heavily to benefit the mother countries.
- Tax Revolts: Heavy taxation led to several notable revolts, including the American Revolution (1775-1783), Comunero Revolt in Colombia (1781), Tupac Amaru Rebellion in Perú (1780-1783), and Mexican War of Independence (1810-1821).

(5) Modern Era (19th Century-Present):
- Industrial Revolution: The rise of industrial economies demanded new paths of taxation, including income taxes and corporate taxes. The U.K.'s Income Tax Act of 1842 marked the beginning of modern income tax systems.
- Progressive Taxation: The concept of progressive taxation, where tax rates increase according to the progression of income, gained traction in the 20th century to address income inequality and to fund social welfare programs.
- Globalization: The integration of global markets led to international tax agreements and efforts to address tax evasion and avoidance by multinational corporations.
- Digital Economy: The rise of the digital economy and e-commerce has prompted new discussions on how to tax digital transactions and the profits of tech giants operating across borders, as well as incomes on intangible properties.

(6) Taxation in the 21st Century:
- Sustainability and Green Taxes: Modern taxation increasingly considers environmental impact, with taxes on carbon emissions and incentives for clean energy as well as increased taxation for fossil fuels.
- International Cooperation: Organizations like the Organisation for Economic Co-operation and Development (OECD) work on frameworks to ensure fair taxation in a globalized economy, addressing issues like base erosion and profit shifting (BEPS).
- Technology and Tax Collection: Developments in technology have improved tax collection and administration, enabling more efficient and transparent systems.

So, from ancient tribute systems to modern tax policies, taxation has been dedicated to supporting state functions, addressing economic needs, and responding to societal changes. And overall, the evolution of taxation reflects wider economic, political, and social changes, as in any other field of History.

And it is interesting to know whether we like it or not but taxes are part of our lives as a society.

b WHY PAY TAXES?

"Taxman" is a song by The Beatles from their 1966 album "Revolver." This catchy song was written by George Harrison and reflected his growing frustration with the high levels of taxation imposed by the British government: in the 1960s, top earners in the U.K., like the Beatles, were liable to a marginal tax rate of up to 95%, referred to as the "super tax." This 95% rate on highest earnings is mentioned in the first verse of "Taxman":

> Let me tell you how it will be, there's one for you, nineteen for me, Cause I'm the Taxman, Yeah, I'm the Taxman. Should five per cent appear too small, be thankful I don't take it all

It is a satirical take on the tax system, with Harrison expressing his discontent with the government's taxation policies. It captures the sentiment of many high-earning individuals of the time who felt the tax rates were excessively burdensome, and it was especially painful to the "Fab Four," who had progressed from working-class people to becoming the biggest musical phenomenon on the planet.

So, they found out that they were earning enormous sums of money but paying most of it straight into the Tax Department. And due to his humble origin, they were not used to paying taxes on this really high percentage.

Opposition to heavy taxation has long been a concern, not only for wealthy artists like The Beatles in the 1960s but also for various individuals throughout history.

Another level of resistance against taxation charged by the United Kingdom in another time and space was one of the main triggers for the American Revolution and, consequently to the independence of the U.S.: the British government wanted to reduce the debt incurred during the French and Indian War (fought between 1754 and 1763) by taxing the American colonies. This was seen as unjust by the colony population on the other side of the Atlantic Ocean, as they felt being unfairly burdened with the cost of a war that primarily benefited British imperial interests.

So, the imposition of taxes by the British government exacerbated existing tensions and contributed to a broader context of political, economic, and social grievances.

In this same context, a mythic figure who had a strong relationship with taxation was Mahatma Gandhi, the anti-colonial activist Indian lawyer. One of the most famous instances of Gandhi's protest against taxation was the Salt March (Dandi March) in 1930: the British government had imposed a heavy tax on salt, a necessity, which disproportionately affected the poor Indian people. The tax laws prohibited Indians from collecting or selling salt independently, forcing them to buy it at high prices from British sources.

Gandhi saw this as an unfair form of taxation that symbolized the larger exploitative nature of British rule. He initiated the Salt March, a 240-mile march to the coastal town of Dandi, where he and his followers symbolically made their own salt by evaporating seawater. This act of rebelliousness gained international attention and became a significant milestone in India's struggle for independence.

Throughout history, heavy taxation has often sparked rebellion, as seen in both the British colonies and colonial Brazil. Minas Conspiracy was a significant (but ultimately unsuccessful) independence movement in colonial Brazil in 1789. The Portuguese crown imposed high taxes on the gold extracted in Minas Gerais, including the quinto (a 20% tax on all gold mined).

When gold production declined, the Portuguese crown continued to demand the same level of tax revenue, leading to widespread economic hardship. The most famous figure of the movement, Tiradentes, was a dentist, military officer, and ardent supporter of independence. He became the symbol of the rebellion, and he is celebrated as a national hero whose execution date, April 21, is a public holiday in Brazil known as Tiradentes Day.

The fairness of taxation is complex and debated, hinging on factors such as equity, the government's role (and services provided to the taxpayers), and the tax system's design.

Nordic countries are known not only for their high tax rates but also for high levels of public trust in government and extensive social safety nets, which many view as just and acceptable due to the balance between taxation and public benefits. However, in many developing nations, tax systems are often seen as unfair due to poor administration, corruption, high levels of evasion, and regressive tax structures that potentially burden the poor more than the rich.

Not surprisingly, taxation was the trigger for several revolts all around the world and at many different times in History. In many cases, the demand for tax justice was tied to broader struggles for political representation, social equality, and economic fairness.

Meanwhile, taxes are fundamental to the adequate functioning of a government. They provide the financial resources necessary for delivering essential public services, maintaining infrastructure, ensuring national security, promoting social equity, and managing economic stability. Without a strong and efficient tax system, governments would struggle to fulfill their roles and responsibilities, leading to potential societal and economic instability.

This is the reason for the inscription engraved on the exterior of the Internal Revenue Services Building in Washington D.C.: "Taxes are what we pay for a civilized society."[1]

Indeed, the purpose of taxation encompasses several key objectives that contribute to the effectiveness and stability of a society. In other words, taxation is the parcel

1. The IRS website credited the remark to the Supreme Court Justice Oliver Wendell Holmes.

of citizens' property which is transferred to the government to provide protection and services provided by the governmental agents.

Evidently, the primary purpose of taxation is to generate revenues for governments, and it is essential for funding public services and infrastructure, such as education, healthcare, transportation, public safety, national defense, law enforcement, and emergency services. Social programs—such as unemployment benefits, social security, and welfare programs that help support vulnerable populations—are also paid by the money from taxation.

Also, governments use taxation as a tool for fiscal policy to influence overall economic activity and achieve macroeconomic goals. Tax policies can be designed to encourage or discourage certain behaviors.

For example, sin taxes on tobacco and alcohol have the purpose of reducing consumption, while tax credits for renewable energy investments stimulate environmentally friendly practices. Or carbon taxes aimed at reducing pollution by making it more costly to emit GHGs.

So, the aim of taxation extends beyond merely raising revenue; it is a vital tool for achieving broader social, economic, and environmental goals. Through effective tax policy, governments can ensure the provision of public goods, promote equity, stabilize the economy, influence behavior, and invest in the future.

An old study published by the International Monetary Fund in 2001[2] gives a good response to the question that opens this chapter by saying that:

> The simple answer is that, until someone comes up with a better idea, taxation is the only practical means of raising the revenue to finance government spending on the goods and services that most of us demand. Setting up an efficient and fair tax system is, however, far from simple, particularly for developing countries that want to become integrated in the international economy. The ideal tax system in these countries should raise essential revenue without excessive government borrowing, and should do so without discouraging economic activity and without deviating too much from tax systems in other countries.

It is a crucial government role. And they have a fiduciary responsibility to use the taxes paid by citizens effectively, transparently, and accountably.

c WELFARE COUNTRIES AND THEIR TAXATION

Governments have a profound responsibility to manage tax revenues judiciously, ensuring that funds are used efficiently, transparently, and equitably to serve the public interest. Governments must commit to accountability, responsiveness, and sustainable fiscal policies, as they foster trust between citizens and their government. By adhering to these principles, governments can uphold their fiduciary duty and ensure that tax revenues contribute to the overall well-being and prosperity of society.

2. Economic Issues No. 27—Tax Policy for Developing Countries (imf.org), https://www.imf.org/external/pubs/ft/issues/issues27/.

As examples of societies under a well-being sentiment and prosperous ones, the Nordic countries (Denmark, Finland, Iceland, Norway, and Sweden) are always mentioned as illustrative examples of welfare states, where governments play a key role in providing social and economic security to their citizens. It has a cost, as approximately half of individuals' total income in the Nordic countries is taxed.

And it raises admiration and challenges for other tax systems around the globe. In a very interesting report about these countries, Deloitte stated that:[3]

> You may be aware of the perks of living in a Nordic country: free and equal access to social services, regardless of income or economic need. That privilege does come at a cost—a marginal tax rate that takes about half a resident's income—but you won't hear most citizens arguing. They're funding the public sector and enjoying a relatively generous social safety net that covers a broad array of services. On top of that, they're reaping the benefits of a well-functioning, competitive economy. This is the case among all the Nordic countries—an extensive, mainly tax-financed welfare system that exists hand-in-hand with a well-functioning economy—and it's such an alluring curiosity to outsiders that it's come to be known as the Nordic paradox. Just how do they do it?
>
> This social welfare model is similarly applied among all the Nordic countries. It has advocates and critics, but discussions often get bogged down by political disagreements and fail to cover the complete picture. For that reason, an evidence-based review of the experience of the Nordic nations can be instructive to executives of government departments and agencies globally, especially those seeking to explore alternative approaches to social services. This report looks at the Nordic model for lessons that are transferable to other societies facing challenges, aiming to generate a dialogue about solutions and reforms that are generally applicable to any public sector in the developed world.

This welfare model is consistently applied across the Nordic countries. While it has advocates and critics, discussions often become targeted in political disagreements without addressing the full picture. For this reason, an evidence-based review of the Nordic experience can be highly instructive for government executives worldwide. Such a review offers lessons that are transferable to other societies facing similar challenges and can generate dialogue about solutions that are applicable to public sectors globally.

The welfare programs available in these countries—such as unemployment benefits, social security, and food assistance—help reduce poverty and provide a safety net for those in need. Universal healthcare improves public health, reduces healthcare costs, and increases life expectancy. Meanwhile, significant investments in public education ensure that all citizens have access to quality learning, which promotes social mobility and economic productivity, as well as equal opportunities for all, regardless of socioeconomic background.

Having said that, Nordic countries are often seen as exemplary models for the integration of environmental protection, social welfare, and good governance that has

3. DI_The-Nordic-social-welfare-model.pdf (deloitte.com), https://www2.deloitte.com/content/dam/insights/us/articles/43149-the-nordic-social-welfare-model/DI_The-Nordic-social-welfare-model.pdf.

allowed these countries to create prosperous, fair, and sustainable societies that serve as models for the world. These countries have developed robust practices for sustainability, social equity, and governance, often leading the global rankings in ESG performance, as follows:

Environmental (E)
- Renewable Energy: Nordic countries are world leaders in renewable energy utilization. For example, Iceland obtains nearly all its electricity from geothermal and hydroelectric sources, while Denmark is a pioneer in wind energy. Nordic countries invest heavily in clean technology and green innovation.
- Low Carbon Footprint: Norway and Sweden have ambitious goals for reducing carbon emissions and have implemented policies like carbon pricing.
- Biodiversity and Conservation: There is a robust thought on preserving natural landscapes and biodiversity. Finland, for example, has enormous national parks and conservation areas.
- Sustainable Cities: Urban planning in cities like Copenhagen and Oslo focuses on sustainability, with widespread bike lanes, efficient public transport systems, and green building standards. Copenhagen aims to become the world's first carbon-neutral capital by 2025.

Social (S)
- Universal Healthcare: High-quality healthcare systems that are accessible to all citizens.
- Education: Free or heavily subsidized education, including higher education, ensures equal opportunities for all.
- Social Security: Comprehensive social safety nets, including unemployment benefits, pensions, and parental leave.
- Gender Equality: High levels of gender equality in the workplace and politics. For instance, Iceland has been leading the Global Gender Gap Index since 2009, and the top five also usually include Nordic countries as long-standing high performers.[4]
- Work-Life Balance: Policies promoting work-life balance, such as generous parental leave and flexible working hours.

Governance (G)
- Low Corruption: Nordic countries consistently rank among the least corrupt nations globally, with transparent government operations and robust legal structures.
- Corporate Governance: Strong corporate governance standards ensure that businesses operate ethically and transparently. Companies are expected to adhere to high standards of social and environmental responsibility, and they operate under a trustable legal system.

4. Index published by the World Economic Forum and available at Global Gender Gap Report 2024 | World Economic Forum (weforum.org), https://www.weforum.org/publications/global-gender-gap-report-2024/digest/.

- Policy Making: Inclusive policymaking processes that involve various stakeholders, ensuring that diverse voices are heard.

Nordic countries have adopted the previously mentioned United Nations SDGs and have made significant progress toward achieving them. It is possible to say that Nordic countries exemplify the principles of ESG through their strong environmental stewardship, comprehensive social welfare systems, and vigorous governance frameworks. By integrating these values into their policies and practices, Nordic countries have achieved high levels of prosperity, social cohesion, and environmental sustainability.

Taxation has played a crucial role in the success of Nordic countries by providing the necessary funding for their comprehensive welfare states, ensuring equitable wealth distribution, and promoting economic stability and growth. And it is characterized by high tax rates and a comprehensive tax structure designed to invest in extensive welfare programs and public services.

Also, it warrants a high degree of income redistribution, as progressive taxation ensures that those who earn higher incomes pay a larger proportion of their income in taxes. This concept rests on the principle of equity, where individuals with higher incomes have a greater ability to contribute to the functioning of society and support its development.

d THE WORST TAX SYSTEMS IN THE WORLD AND THEIR DAMAGE TO ESG AGENDA

In contrast to progressive taxation, largely applied to Nordic countries, regressive taxation is a system where the tax rate decreases (or remains the same) as the taxable amount increases. To put it another way, poorer individuals pay a higher percentage of their income in taxes compared to richer individuals.

This type of taxation disproportionately and negatively affects lower-income earners, so it places a greater burden on them. These flawed systems contribute to economic inequality and hinder efforts to address environmental, social, and governance (ESG) goals.

Besides being regressive, the "worst" taxation systems are typically characterized by high complexity, inefficiency, corruption, and economic instability. These issues weaken the ability of governments to collect taxes effectively and to provide public services, leading to dissatisfaction and noncompliance among taxpayers.

Therefore, these bad tax system has some common topics: intricate tax codes and bureaucratic procedures, thus making compliance complicated and costly for taxpayers; high tax rates together with flawed and inadequate public services that lead to dissatisfaction and rebellions; frequent economic crises and inflation, leading to erratic and unstable tax and macroeconomic environments; high levels of corruption and government misconduct; and widespread tax evasion and a large informal sector limit the tax base and place a disproportionate burden on compliant taxpayers.

As published by the Tax Foundation website:[5]

> The structure of a country's tax code is a determining factor of its economic performance. A well-structured tax code is easy for taxpayers to comply with and can promote economic development while raising sufficient revenue for a government's priorities. In contrast, poorly structured tax systems can be costly, distort economic decision-making, and harm domestic economies.

Because of all these topics above, bad tax systems are difficult to implement ESG agenda in several ways because:

- Lack of Revenue: Inefficient tax systems often fail to generate adequate revenue, leading to underfunding of environmental protection and sustainability programs.
- Misallocation of Funds: Funds meant for environmental initiatives may be diverted for other purposes due to corruption.
- Failure to Incentivize Green Practices: Poorly designed tax systems may lack effective environmental taxes (like carbon taxes), failing to stimulate businesses and individuals to implement environmentally friendly practices.
- Pollution and Resource Depletion: Without proper environmental taxes and regulations, companies may continue polluting and depleting natural resources without bearing the true environmental costs.
- Regressive Tax Structures: Ineffective tax systems often result in regressive taxation, where the poor pay a higher proportion of their income compared to the wealthy, worsening social gaps.
- Undermining Social Services: Insufficient tax revenue leads to underfunded public services such as healthcare, infrastructure, education, and social security, harming the most vulnerable populations.
- Social Unrest: Inequitable and inefficient tax systems can lead to social unrest and instability, as citizens feel the burden of taxes without seeing corresponding benefits in public services.
- Corruption: Corruption in tax collection and allocation undermines good governance, leading to a lack of transparency and accountability, making it difficult for citizens to understand how their taxes are being used.
- Inefficiency: Bureaucratic inefficiency and complex tax regulations create administrative burdens and opportunities for corruption, reducing the effectiveness of governance.

The current situation in Venezuela comprises all the topics above, as local tax system is widely considered problematic and has significant weaknesses that reflect the country's broader economic and political challenges, such as:

- Years of economic mismanagement, including price controls and nationalization of industries, stagnated the economy and reduced the tax base.

5. 2023 International Tax Competitiveness Index | Tax Foundation, https://taxfoundation.org/research/all/global/2023-international-tax-competitiveness-index/.

- Persistent political instability and lack of confidence in government institutions.
- Complex tax code that is frequently changed in response to economic conditions, making compliance difficult for businesses and individuals.
- Last but not least, rampant corruption, with tax officials often demanding bribes, which undermines the integrity and effectiveness of the tax system.

Therefore, the tax system in Venezuela is thwarted by a combination of economic mismanagement, political instability, corruption, complexity, and inadequate enforcement. The deficient performance of the tax system is both a cause and a symptom of the broader economic and political crisis facing the country.

Evidently, taxation is only one of the problems faced by the Venezuelan people. This country is a typical example of the syndrome named by the economist as "oil curse" that happens when a country becomes overwhelmed by the fabulous wealth produced by petroleum while ignoring other economic areas, preferring to maximize the windfall generated by oil. This phenomenon characteristically leads to heightened political, social and economic dysfunction due to ineffective governance and wild corruption.

As another local tax problem, local Value Added Tax (VAT) is high (16% rate), which tends to bring regressivity to the system, as it places a disproportionate burden on lower-income individuals. Then, as this sales tax is uniformly applicable to all consumers based on what they buy, even though the tax rate is uniform at 16%, lower-income consumers are more affected.

To illustrate it, let's imagine two individuals and each one purchases USD 100 of food per week, so each of them pays USD 16 in tax on their food purchases:

- The first individual earns USD 2,000 per week, making the sales tax rate on his purchase 0.8% of income.
- In contrast, the other individual earns USD 320 per week, making his food sales tax represent 5% of his income.

Although the tax rate is the same in both cases, the person with the lower income pays a higher percentage of income.

Bad tax systems are awful for society because they usually do not comply with the simple rules cited above. Consequently, they harm the ESG agenda by failing to provide adequate funding for environmental and social programs, exacerbating social inequality, and undermining good governance.

As seen in the example of Nordic countries, effective tax systems are crucial for achieving ESG goals, as they ensure equitable distribution of resources, reduce gaps in education opportunities, support sustainable development, and promote transparency and accountability in governance.

Adam Smith, an 18th-century Scottish economist, philosopher, and author who is deemed as the father of modern economics, claimed in his 1776 seminal book, "The Wealth of Nations," that tax policy should follow four principles: fairness, certainty, convenience and efficiency. These four principles have been broadly accepted as the foundations of a well-functioning tax system. And none of them are seen in "tax nightmares" countries.

e LAFFER CURVE AND DIGITAL NOMADISM

When it comes to the government and taxes, it often feels like too much tax is never enough. But there is indeed a measure utilized to present just how much the government can take from taxpayers' wallet: the Laffer Curve.

It represents an economic theory that illustrates the relationship between tax rates and tax revenue obtained by the Tax government. Named after economist Arthur Laffer, the curve indicates that there is an optimal tax rate that maximizes government revenue. The basic premise is that as tax rates increase from low levels, tax revenue also increases, but only up to a certain point. Beyond this point, additional increases in tax rates lead to a decrease in tax revenue.

In other words, at low-tax rates, increasing the tax rate leads to an increase in tax revenue. This is because the tax rate is still low enough that it does not significantly discourage people from working, investing, or spending. However, if tax rates continue to rise beyond the revenue-maximizing point, tax revenue begins to decrease. This happens because higher tax rates can discourage economic activities like work, investment, and consumption, leading to lower taxable income and thus lower tax revenue.

The Laffer Curve is based on the idea that individuals and businesses respond to tax incentives. Higher reductions might lead to reduced work effort, increased tax avoidance and tax evasion, all of which reduce the overall tax base.

Policymakers working on mature tax systems can use the concepts together to design taxes that not only correct for social costs but also consider the impact on revenue and economic activity, even though the Laffer Curve does not specify the exact rate where revenue is maximized and this rate can differ depending on the economic context, making it difficult to apply in practice. In other words, what percentage is the proper balance between tax revenue and employee incentivization achieved?

Talking about the example cited by the "Taxman" song, if a government imposes such a very high tax rate for Income Tax (95%), reducing the rate might lead to more people working and consequently earning taxable income, thereby increasing the tax base and total revenue. On the contrary, if the tax rate is very low (say 10%), increasing it could raise more revenue without significantly discouraging economic activity.

Expanding this rationale, at 0%, there would be no tax revenue since none is collected; at 100%, there is no revenue since no one would work solely to pay taxes.

In summary, the Laffer Curve illustrates that there is a trade-off between tax rates and tax revenue, and finding the optimal tax rate is crucial for maximizing government revenue without stifling economic growth.

Going one step further, if a tax is extremely high—i.e., situated on an extreme point on the Laffer Curve—and takes a substantial portion of income or wealth, not only the potential evasion will occur, but it can also represent a barrier to innovation because innovators, entrepreneurs, and investors often take significant risks with the hope of achieving high returns.

Confiscatory taxes reduce the potential high after-tax return on successful innovations, making risk-taking less attractive, as rewards may not justify the risks involved. Also, innovation typically requires substantial investment in research and development.

Also, confiscatory taxes can reduce the available capital for such investments, both from private investors and from retained earnings within companies. The relationship between confiscatory taxes and the Laffer Curve illustrates that there are practical limits to how much revenue can be raised through taxation. Extremely high tax rates can be counterproductive, leading to less, not more, revenue.

Additionally, in a globalized economy, talents and capital are mobile and fluid. Regions with confiscatory taxes may lose their competitive edge as innovators seek more attractive environments elsewhere.

As more professionals adopt the digital nomad lifestyle, high tax jurisdictions may experience a loss of talent and revenue, further complicating tax policy decisions.

Note that digital nomadism allows individuals to work from anywhere, as access to diverse cultural perspectives and expertise can drive innovation by bringing together different ideas and problem-solving approaches.

And high taxes might drive innovators, entrepreneurs, and highly skilled workers to relocate to jurisdictions with more favorable tax environments. This "brain drain" can reduce the innovative capacity of the region by imposing confiscatory taxes.

High taxation in one's home country can incentivize individuals to seek tax-friendly jurisdictions. Digital nomads, who are not tied to a specific location, can move to countries with lower tax rates, favorable tax treaties, or special tax regimes designed for remote workers. This ability to optimize tax obligations is a significant driver for some people to adopt the digital nomad lifestyle.

Spain, for example, has introduced the Spanish Digital Nomad Visa, also known as the Spain Remote Work Visa, aiming to attract remote workers, freelancers, and digital nomads from outside the European Economic Area to live and work in Spain. It is part of the country's effort to stimulate the economy and capitalize on the growing trend of remote work. It permitted the ones under this visa to live and work in Spain for up to 12 months initially, with the possibility of renewal for up to five years.

Spain is not alone. Several other countries have similar possibilities for sheltering overseas tax residents, such as Barbados, Costa Rica, Georgia, Portugal, Malta, Estonia and Croatia. As this is a growing reality because of the digital economy, countries with high tax rates may experience a decline in their tax base, particularly if wealthy individuals or skilled professionals leave.

Dubai case is relevant to mention, as the United Arab Emirates offers a Virtual Working Program, allowing remote workers and their families to live in the country for up to one year while working remotely for foreign companies. What makes it most significant is the fact that Dubai has no personal income tax, making it an attractive destination for digital nomads who want to minimize their tax obligations.

In this regard, this fluid mobility is another criticism of the Laffer curve: it means a static form of analysis, since it does not reflect how individuals and businesses can adapt their behavior. It considers one set of variables, but the model tends to focus mainly on aggregated tax revenue without pondering the nuanced differences between various industries (e.g., big tech companies and their wealth based on intangibles) and individuals (as digital nomadism cases).

In any case, Laffer Curve's teachings show us that this potential loss of revenue due to confiscatory taxation can lead to a reduction in taxes collected and to challenges for governments trying to maintain public services and social programs.

Also, it can hinder the search for innovative ideas, something fundamental for the times we are living in.

f THE CORNER WHERE TAXES, GREEN AGENDA, IKIGAI AND VICTOR FRANKL MEET

Climate change is a global concern, prompting discussions among governments, international organizations, multinational corporations, and even individuals in daily conversations about ways to mitigate its impact.

Despite all the political considerations about ESG (and the previously commented backlash), transition to a sustainability agenda is the pathway for reducing poverty, protecting the planet and attacking inequalities.

Also, the challenges arising from an aging global population (and the necessary public health systems jointly with Social Security care) and the quick depletion of natural resources have made sustainability a more pressing topic than ever before. Accomplishing the goal of making the world more sustainable has become an economic, political, and social priority.

To achieve this objective, taxation plays a crucial role: green taxation is a multifaceted term and comprises both the stick of higher taxes for activities that are not friendly to the environment and the carrot of incentives and subsidies for green behaviors. The most common sticks and carrots for green taxation are:

(1) Carbon Taxes: By imposing taxes levied on carbon emissions, governments can incentivize businesses and individuals to reduce their carbon footprint. This encourages investment in cleaner technologies and energy sources.
(2) Subsidies and Tax Credits: Offering tax breaks or subsidies for renewable energy projects (like full depreciation in the year of acquisition) and energy-efficient appliances can foster their adoption. This makes green alternatives more money-wise attractive compared to conventional options.
(3) Pollution Taxes: Like carbon taxes, taxes on other forms of pollution (e.g., plastic waste and water pollutants) can persuade industries to adopt cleaner processes and reduce their environmental impact.
(4) Land Use and Development Taxes: Implementing taxes on land use that promote urban extension or deforestation can encourage more sustainable development practices, such as the preservation of green spaces.

(5) Reinvestment of Tax Revenue: Revenue obtained from environmental taxes can be reinvested into green projects, such as public transportation infrastructure, renewable energy research, and conservation programs.
(6) Vehicle Taxes: Imposing higher taxes on vehicles with poor fuel efficiency and providing tax incentives for ethanol (or other clean energy, like biomass) fueled may shift consumer behavior towards greener transportation options.
(7) Green Bonds and Investments: Tax incentives for green bonds can encourage investments in sustainable projects, such as renewable energy plants, green buildings, and sustainable agriculture.
(8) Waste Management Taxes: Taxes on landfill use and incentives for recycling can promote better waste management practices and reduce the environmental burden of waste, as well as promote a circular economy.
(9) International Cooperation: Taxation policies can be organized internationally to address global environmental challenges, ensuring that companies do not simply relocate to countries with lax environmental regulations. The European Carbon Border Adjustment Mechanism (CBAM) (to be discussed afterwards) is an interesting example of this carbon escape control policy.

Item 1 previously mentioned, i.e., the imposition of carbon taxes to reflect the environmental and social cost of carbon, is universally understood as an essential policy tool to restrain carbon emissions, as higher prices for carbon-emitting goods will lower demand for them. This type of tax is usually charged over fossil fuels.

Some jurisdictions have already adopted such a tax, and Finland was the first country to implement a carbon tax. Finland introduced its carbon tax in 1990, setting a precedent for other nations to follow in using fiscal policy as a tool to combat GHG emissions. The tax initially focused on the carbon content of fossil fuels, and over time, it has been adjusted to address environmental goals more effectively.

Note the idea of implementing a carbon tax may not be a panacea: its welfare impacts may mostly affect poor people, as a tax on fossil fuels tends to be more regressive, since:

(i) lower-income families tend to spend a larger share of their income on energy-related expenses, such as heating, electricity, and transportation. Lower-income families often have fewer options to switch to greener, more energy-efficient alternatives due to the upfront costs involved; and
(ii) higher fuel prices can lead to increased costs for goods and services as companies will transfer these additional costs to their consumers. This can result in a higher cost of living, which disproportionately impacts those with lower incomes, as they have less financial flexibility.

Within this context, it is notable that the United Nations' actions aim to assist poor countries in implementing a tax policy whose purpose is to lead to decarbonization. As published on the "Tax for SDGs" initiative website:[6]

6. About: UNDP Tax for SDGs, https://www.taxforsdgs.org/about.

> The Tax for Sustainable Development Goals Initiative, or Tax for SDGs, supports developing countries in increasing domestic resource mobilization (DRM) and achieving the Sustainable Development Goals (SDGs). Under the Initiative, taxation is considered both a tool for revenue collection and a policy instrument to encourage sustainable growth strategies and influence behaviour towards desired outcomes related to climate, nature, well-being, and governance.
>
> Tax for SDGs leverages UNDP's role as an enabler, integrator and catalyst at the country level. It works to expand people's choices for a fairer, sustainable future with planet and people in balance and achieve the vision of the world as set out in the 2030 Agenda for Sustainable Development.

By strategically using taxation tools, governments can establish a financial landscape that supports and accelerates the transition to a greener economy. Thus, governments may utilize plenty of targeted policies and fiscal mechanisms to coordinate this "green adjustment" across different market segments.

This is the tax agent's side; this is the view of the tax authorities.

Talking about the professional who works with taxation, the ones who can find the intersections between passion, skills, societal needs, and professional opportunities within the field of taxation, leading to a more fulfilling and purposeful career than allying work with personal "ikigai," since tax profession can be:

(1) Aligned with Passion:
  - Social Equity: If you care about social justice or environmental issues, focusing on making tax systems more equitable and reducing the regressive impacts of taxes can be your driving passion, as well as incorporating tax incentives into the green agenda as part of the day-by-day activities.

(2) Utilizing Skills:
  - Analytical Skills: Tax work often involves complex data analysis, financial wisdom, problem solving and understanding of economic principles. If you are skilled in these areas, this can be a strong component of your ikigai. Or, if your personal skills are more linked to a strong communication capacity, educating suppliers, clients, your team, and the community about tax regulations can be rewarding.

(3) Serving a Mission:
  - Public Good: Taxation is essential for funding public services and infrastructure. Your work contributes to the common good, ensuring that governments have the resources to provide infrastructure, healthcare, education, and other vital services.

(4) Earning a Living:
  - Professional Fulfillment: A career in taxation can be financially rewarding and offer job security because taxation is a fundamental aspect of all economies. Knowing that your work is valued and compensated can complete the professional aspect of ikigai.

(5) Mentorship and Education:

  - For those passionate about teaching and guiding others, the tax profession offers many opportunities to mentor young professionals or educate businesses and individuals on tax matters. Sharing knowledge can provide deep personal satisfaction.

(6) Boost Economic Development:

  - Tax profession allows to contribute to national and global economic stability. Adequate tax policy is essential for a healthy economy, and tax professionals are key in advising governments on fiscal policies that help shape tax policies aiming to encourage entrepreneurship, foreign investment, and job creation.
  - Also, working with international organizations to assist developing countries in establishing fair tax systems that can support economic growth can be a journey full of purpose.

Altogether, it encompasses the ikigai idea and Frankl's lessons: to inspire a workplace culture that values purpose and contribution over solely chasing profit and personal wealth.

Companies that focus on meaningful goals, such as innovation, social impact, and a positive effect on environment, often find that success and profitability follow naturally.

And a happier team will be a pleasant and natural part of this process.

CHAPTER 4
Tax Policy

a CHICKEN TAX

As Benjamin Franklin famously observed, "nothing can be said to be certain, except death and taxes."

This reflects the universal truth that all human beings will die. It highlights the inevitability of mortality, something no one can avoid. And the second part of the sentence refers to the unavoidable nature of taxes. Regardless of one's financial situation, background, or status, everyone is subject to taxes in some form, making it an unavoidable part of life, especially in societies with structured governments.

Indeed, taxes have played a fundamental role in shaping the world economy, our lives as a community administered by governments and our societal behavior.

And this chapter will explore how taxes not only fund government services but also influence global industries, consumer behavior, and economic growth.

From funding public goods and redistributing wealth to regulating behavior and influencing global trade, taxation has been instrumental in the development of modern societies.

Taxation is a powerful tool that governments use not only to raise revenue but also to outline societal values, economic structures, and the overall well-being of the population.

Also, taxes are present in our day-to-day lives, and several cases can be brought up in different countries and situations.

A picturesque example of taxation affecting comportment occurs in the United Kingdom: local VAT is charged at 20% on most products sold to consumers, but some essential products, including food and children's clothes, are exempt. So, this exception to children's clothing has persuaded some petite adult women to purchase their apparel in the teen sector of department stores. Just to illustrate the case herein, the measures for children's clothing are established by U.K. Tax Authorities on their website,[1] and it encompasses chest measures of 105 cm for girls' clothing.

Another quaint case in the United Kingdom is the tax classification of Pringles potato chips: there was a controversy about whether Pringles should be categorized as "potato crisps," which are subject to VAT, or as a general food product because most of them are exempt from VAT. Initially, in 2008, the court ruled in favor of Procter & Gamble (Pringle's producer), stating it is not potato crisps, thus making them VAT-exempt. However, in 2009, the Court of Appeal overturned this decision, ruling that despite their differences, Pringles were still "potato crisps or potato-based snacks" and therefore subject to VAT.

These cases are very interesting, but the one to be commented on in this chapter has more to do with macroeconomics, trade barriers and taxation's long-lasting effects: it is the denominated "Chicken Tax" and refers to a 25% tariff imposed by the U.S. on imported light trucks, including pickup trucks and vans. This tariff, which dates to the early 1960s, has had significant and lasting effects on the American automotive market.

After World War II, the U.S. and European economies were rebuilding and expanding. As part of this recovery, trade between the U.S. and Europe increased, including the export and import of various goods. In this context, the switch to automated factory farming in the U.S. transformed chicken from a luxury food to a mass-produced product.

Once American poultry companies had satisfied the domestic demand, they started shipping their surplus across the Atlantic. By the late 1950s and early 1960s, American poultry producers had intensely increased their exports of chicken to Europe, especially to West Germany.

The influx of cheap American chicken was identified as a risk to local European poultry industries. In response, several European countries, led by France and West Germany, imposed tariffs and other restrictions on U.S. chicken imports. The French government prohibited U.S. chicken and raised concerns that hormones could influence male virility, while German farmers' associations accused North American poultry companies of artificially fattening chicken by using a powerful poison named arsenic. Subsequently, the Dutch government accused the U.S. of dumping chickens at prices below their cost.

In 1962, the European Commission adopted the Common Agricultural Policy, imposing minimum import prices on all imported chicken and invalidating prior tariff bindings and concessions.

In retaliation for these European tariffs and costs on American poultry, the U.S. government in 1963, under President Lyndon B. Johnson, implemented tariffs on several imported goods. One of the most significant was a 25% tariff on imported light trucks, which included pickup trucks and vans.

This tariff was mainly aimed at Germany—where a collection of innovative and economical small vans and pickups were produced, and Volkswagen was gaining market share in the U.S. with its van Type 2 (also known as the VW Bus or Kombi).

1. Young children's clothing and footwear (VAT Notice 714)—GOV.UK (www.gov.uk), https://www.gov.uk/guidance/vat-on-young-childrens-clothing-and-footwear-notice-714.

This tariff became known as the "Chicken Tax."

Although the original dispute over chicken exports was later resolved, the tariff on light trucks remained in place, and it effectively protected American automakers, particularly Ford, General Motors, and Chrysler, from foreign competition in the pickup truck market.

This safeguard allowed U.S. manufacturers to dominate the domestic market for decades and made it financially unviable for foreign automakers to export light trucks to the U.S. market. As a result, even non-European companies like Toyota, Nissan, and Honda—which later became important players in the American automotive market—encountered significant barriers to entering the light truck segment.

It is curious to note that some foreign manufacturers found imaginative ways to bypass the Chicken Tax. For example, certain vehicles were imported as passenger vehicles with seats installed and were then transformed into light trucks once they reached the U.S. These vehicles were categorized differently to avoid the tariff. Also, it inspired "tariff engineering" procedures by manufacturers disassembling, importing, and assembling vehicles already in the U.S. to avoid the tax.

But the U.S. government closed many of these loopholes afterwards.

The Chicken Tax remains in place today, and its effects can be felt in the U.S. automotive market. While the tariff no longer plays the same role it did in the past, it has strongly affected the landscape of the American auto industry by ensuring that light trucks remained largely the domain of domestic manufacturers.

So, the supremacy of American light trucks in the U.S. market is partially explained by this conflict and the resulting tax. And this is a remarkable example of how trade policies can have long-lasting and unexpected influences on global trade and manufacturing strategies across distinct industries and jurisdictions, shaping markets and industries for decades.

As an additional comment, many American-made trucks, which have long benefited from this protective tariff, are now manufactured in Mexico and Canada, as these countries frequently benefit from a preferential tariff treatment under the United States-Mexico and Canada Agreement, formerly known as North American Free Trade Agreement, that grants a more fluid movement of goods and vehicles across North American borders.

In any case, it is noteworthy how "Chicken Tax" shaped the automotive industry in the U.S., guaranteeing the supremacy of American-made trucks.

b THE IMPORTANCE OF TAXATION, ECONOMIC GROWTH AND THE 2017 U.S. TAX REFORM

Tax is a fundamental mechanism for the economic story of a country, as we had seen in the previous chapter. Also, it reflects and shapes the society it is embedded in.

Tax policy and economic growth are intimately connected, as tax policies can significantly influence economic behavior, resource allocation, and overall economic performance of a given nation. It may happen in several ways:

(1) Impact on Incentives and Investment:
- Tax Rates on Income and Profits: High taxes on personal income, corporate profits, or capital gains can reduce the incentive for people and companies to work, invest, and innovate. Conversely, lower taxes can stimulate investment by raising the after-tax income on direct investment, leading to more capital formation, new ideas through investment in innovation, and economic growth. Competitive corporate tax rates can attract foreign investment, while high rates may drive businesses to relocate to more tax-friendly jurisdictions, influencing domestic job creation and, consequently, economic growth.
- Tax Incentives: Governments often use tax incentives (e.g., deductions, credits, accelerated depreciation) to encourage specific activities like research and development (R&D), renewable energy investments, or capital expenditures. These incentives can spike innovation and productivity, contributing to economic growth.

(2) Consumption and Demand:
- Consumption Taxes: Sales taxes, VATs, and excise taxes directly affect consumer prices. Higher consumption taxes can reduce consumer spending, while lower taxes may increase disposable income and stimulate demand for goods and services, boosting economic growth.
- Behavioral Responses: Changes in tax policy can influence consumer behavior. For example, a tax cut might lead to increased spending, while a tax increase could lead to more savings or reduced consumption, affecting overall economic activity.

(3) Distribution of Income and Wealth:
- Progressive v. Regressive Taxes: Tax policy affects income distribution. Progressive taxes (higher rates on higher incomes) can reduce income inequality, potentially leading to a more stable society, which can be conducive to growth. However, overly progressive taxes (as the U.K. 95% tax sung by The Beatles in "Taxman") might discourage high earners from investing or working as much. And it may trigger the exodus of wealthy people to low taxation jurisdictions.
- Social Equity and Stability: Tax policies that reduce inequality may contribute to social stability, which is important for sustained economic growth. However, if taxes are perceived as unfair or too onerous, they can lead to tax evasion, lower compliance, and reduced economic efficiency.

(4) Deficit Financing and Debt:
- Deficit Spending: When tax revenues are not enough to cover government spending, governments often borrow to finance the deficit. While some levels of deficit spending can stimulate growth, excessive debt can lead to higher interest rates, hindering private investment, and in the end, reduce economic growth, as the interests will be too high to contract new investments.

- Tax Policy and Fiscal Sustainability: Sustainable tax policies that balance revenue and spending without excessive borrowing promote long-term economic stability and growth. Unsustainable tax policies, on the other hand, can lead to fiscal crises that undermine economic growth.

(5) Long-Term Economic Growth:

- Structural Tax Reforms: Tax policies that encourage long-term investments in human capital, technology, and infrastructure can lead to sustained economic growth. Structural reforms that simplify the tax code and reduce distortions in economic decision-making can enhance efficiency and productivity.
- Sustainability: Environmentally oriented tax policies can promote sustainable economic growth by encouraging businesses and consumers to adopt cleaner technologies and practices, as well as innovation towards green agenda.

Therefore, tax policy is a powerful tool that models economic incentives, resource allocation, and overall economic dynamics. The design and implementation of tax policy can either promote or hinder economic growth, depending on how it affects investment, consumption, government spending, and the overall economic environment. Effective tax policies strike a balance between generating necessary government revenue and fostering an environment conducive to sustained economic growth.

Some examples of successful tax systems may be encountered in Economic literature (Switzerland, Estonia, Singapore, Hong Kong, New Zealand, etc.) with a common feature of being simple tax methodologies. All these jurisdictions are indeed good examples of healthy tax administrations helping the growth of the economy. Things get a lot more complicated to evaluate when the analysis considers bigger countries with more political divisions and several interests around them.

An illustrative case is the 2017 U.S. tax reform, officially known as the Tax Cuts and Jobs Act (TCJA). It was a significant overhaul of the U.S. tax code, and one of its key objectives was to make the U.S. a more attractive destination for investment.

Its main power was the reduction of the corporate tax rate from 35% to 21%. This significant cut made the U.S. more competitive on the global stage, encouraging both U.S. and foreign companies to invest in the U.S. rather than in lower-tax jurisdictions.

But another important new regulation was foreseen by TCJA, as follows.

Before TCJA, the U.S. functioned under a worldwide tax system, meaning U.S. companies were taxed on their global earnings, with the capacity to defer taxes on foreign profits until they were repatriated to the U.S. This led many North American companies to keep profits abroad to avoid higher U.S. taxes, reducing domestic investment.

The TCJA introduced a territorial tax system, where U.S. companies are generally only taxed on their domestic profits, with exemptions for most foreign profits. This shift eliminated the incentive for companies to keep profits offshore, encouraging them to repatriate funds and reinvest them in the U.S.

Repatriation of profits was another attractive possibility granted by TCJA through the one-time Repatriation Tax to the trillions of dollars in profits held by U.S. companies overseas to avoid high U.S. taxes upon repatriation. TCJA included a one-time mandatory repatriation tax on these accumulated overseas profits at a reduced rate of 15.5% for cash and 8% for non-cash assets. This provision led to a significant influx of capital back to the U.S., which could be used for investment, stock buybacks, dividends, or debt repayment.

The 2017 U.S. tax reform, by reducing the corporate tax rate, transitioning to a territorial tax system, and providing various incentives for investment, significantly enhanced the attractiveness of the U.S. as a destination for both domestic and foreign investment.

It achieved some short-term economic stimulus, made U.S. corporate taxes more competitive, and simplified aspects of the tax code. However, it also impacted significantly the national deficit, aggravated wealth inequality, and provided relatively limited long-term benefits for the middle class. So, critics may correctly argue that TCJA was the biggest contributor to the large increase in the deficit.

In any case, its changes contributed to increased capital inflows, higher levels of business investment, and overall economic growth by enhancing the global competitiveness of U.S. multinationals.

And this is an example of how taxation can effectively contribute to economic activity.

c REVENUE GENERATION, TAXATION AND THE "FEELGOOD" ATTITUDE

The enormous tax reductions granted by the TCJA reached its macroeconomic objectives. But it led to an issue: an enormous budget deficit. It happens because lowering taxes without a corresponding decrease in spending can increase the deficit, as it reduces the revenue available to cover government expenditures.

Taxes are the primary source of revenue for governments. They fund public services, infrastructure, social programs, defense, and other government expenditures. So, a budget deficit occurs when the total government's expenditure to provide these services exceeds its revenues (basically taxes) in a given fiscal period, typically a year. This shortfall must be covered by borrowing, usually through the issuance of government bonds.

When a government runs a deficit, it may need to increase taxes in the future to pay off the debt and interest incurred from borrowing. Conversely, if the government raises taxes now, it can reduce the need for borrowing and, therefore, the size of future deficits.

Going beyond, when a government borrows to cover a deficit, it must ultimately repay that debt. This can lead to higher taxes in the future, as the government needs to produce sufficient revenue to service its debt. Persistent deficits can lead to a growing national debt, which may require even higher taxes or reduced spending in the future to manage the debt burden.

This book is not about politics, but it is worth mentioning that different political ideologies have contrasting views on the appropriate levels of taxation and acceptable deficits. Some may prioritize reducing deficits through spending cuts, while others may focus on increasing taxes, particularly on higher-income individuals or corporations, to balance the budget.

Thus, taxation and deficits are interconnected through government revenue and spending decisions. Managing this relationship is crucial for maintaining economic stability, promoting growth, and ensuring fiscal responsibility. Of course, money stolen through corruption schemes is an awful component of this equation, thus affecting this balance.

Talking again about the TCJA of 2017, it significantly increased fiscal deficits in the U.S. because it triggered a significant reduction in federal revenue. Proponents of the TCJA argued that the tax cuts would spur economic growth, which in turn would generate additional tax revenue and offset some of the lost revenue from the cuts.

A similar effect occurred in the U.S. when President Ronald Reagan implemented major tax cuts through the Economic Recovery Tax Act (ERTA) of 1981, also known as the "Reagan tax cuts." At the time, the U.S. was experiencing high inflation and unemployment, leading to a period of economic stagnation. ERTA lowered the top marginal individual income tax rate from 70% to 50%, reduced the lowest tax bracket from 14% to 11% and offered significant tax relief for businesses by providing incentives for capital investment.

Among ERTA impacts, the U.S. economy grew substantially during the 1980s, experiencing an average Gross Domestic Product growth rate of 3.5% per year, and unemployment fell from a peak of 10.8% in 1982 to 5.3% by 1989. Nevertheless, these tax cuts significantly increased the budget deficit, and critics argue that the economic growth was also fueled by other factors, such as the loosening of monetary policy.

An analogous debate was held during Margaret Thatcher's years in the United Kingdom, as she implemented a series of tax cuts: Thatcher government significantly reduced the top personal income tax rate from 83% to 60% in 1979 and later to 40% in 1988 (far from the 95% rate sung by The Beatles). Corporate taxes were also reduced, and the basic rate of income tax was cut from 33% to 25% during her tenure. Also, Thatcher privatized state-owned industries, including British Telecom, British Gas, British Airways and electricity companies, putting them into private hands.

Initially, these tax cuts led to a reduction in government revenue, contributing to higher deficits, especially in the early 1980s. The government sought to offset the revenue loss by increasing VAT and cutting public spending. However, the deficit rose in the early 1980s, partly due to the recession and rising unemployment, before the economy began to recover later in the decade. As clearly explained in a BBC article:[2]

> With money from tax cuts in their pockets, shoppers began to rediscover the "feelgood factor". They were encouraged further as credit was unleashed.

2. Margaret Thatcher: How her changes affected your finances—BBC News, https://www.bbc.com/news/business-22064354.

> Restrictions on hire purchase offers were relaxed, stores offered credit, credit cards boomed. Consumer borrowing tripled during the 1980s.
>
> And, of course, mortgages were easier to get. The old rule of thumb that you only borrow two-and-a-half times salary was thrown out of the window.
>
> Building societies were allowed to lend more and foreign banks set up in the UK to compete.
>
> The Bank of England did not control the expansion of credit and there are those who see the roots of the current financial crisis in the credit boom of the Thatcher years.

Between 2012 and 2020, Japan faced a similar question as a result of economic policies under Prime Minister Shinzo Abe, often referred to as "Abenomics": as part of efforts to stimulate economic growth, the Abe government reduced the corporate tax rate from 38% in 2012 to 30% by 2016, with further reductions in subsequent years. The goal was to encourage investment and improve Japan's global competitiveness.

While these tax cuts were aimed at stimulating the economy, they also contributed to Japan's already high fiscal deficits due to slow economic growth, an aging population, and high social welfare spending. As explained in Bloomberg:[3]

> Japan's Prime Minister Shinzo Abe had a bold strategy: shock therapy for an economy that had been stagnant for 20 years and was overtaken by China as the world's second-largest in 2010. Launched three years later, Abenomics, as the doctrine is known, departed from the piecemeal measures of previous leaders and antagonized powerful political constituencies. Abe told voters that the strong economic medicine was Japan's last chance to remain a world power, framing his policies as a matter of national security. Progress was patchy at best, however, even before the hammer blow of the Covid-19 pandemic—and Abe's decision to step down after a record-setting eight-year run.

As occurred in the Japanese case seen above, an aging population can have a profound impact on fiscal deficits by increasing government spending on pensions, healthcare, and social security, while simultaneously reducing revenue due to a shrinking labor force and slower economic growth.

Also, high government wages and benefits for public sector employees can lead to increased spending; government subsidies to industries, agriculture, or energy; significant expenditures on defense and military operations and large-scale infrastructure projects, such as building roads, bridges, and airports, require significant capital outlay, which can strain government finances.

External shocks, i.e., events like earthquakes, floods, or pandemics, can lead to sudden increases in government spending on disaster relief and reconstruction while also reducing revenue; a global economic downturn (as happened because of COVID-19) can reduce export revenues and foreign investment, impacting government revenue and leading to a fiscal deficit.

3. How the Shock Therapy of "Abenomics" Worked in Japan: QuickTake—Bloomberg, https://www.bloomberg.com/news/articles/2020-08-28/how-the-shock-therapy-of-abenomics-worked-in-japan-quicktake.

So, a fiscal deficit results from the complex interplay of high public expenditures, reduced government revenues, economic cycles, demographic shifts, and policy decisions. Addressing a fiscal deficit often requires a combination of measures, including spending cuts, revenue enhancements, and structural reforms, to ensure long-term fiscal sustainability.

During periods of strong economic growth, tax revenues typically rise as businesses earn more profits, individuals make higher incomes, and consumption grows. This leads to higher collections from income taxes, corporate taxes, and sales taxes, contributing to a fiscal surplus if expenditures are controlled.

This economic growth can also create a multiplier effect, where increased government revenue from taxes is reinvested into the economy, further stimulating growth and increasing tax receipts.

This is the "dream situation" for any government: fiscal surplus, increased investor confidence, potentially increasing tax revenue through higher investment and economic growth. And taxation duly balanced has a vital role in this optimal position by triggering the "feelgood" sentiment for the people, i.e., "a feeling among ordinary people that everything is going well, and that they do not need to worry about losing their jobs or spending money."[4]

However, the functions driven by taxation go beyond the mere raising of financial resources to governments. And this is the topic to be covered in the next section of this book.

d BEHAVIORAL INFLUENCE AND PIGOUVIAN TAXES

Arthur Cecil Pigou was an English economist and a teacher and builder of the School of Economics at the University of Cambridge. In his book "The Economics of Welfare," Pigou developed the concept of externalities, i.e., costs or benefits presented by others that are not considered by the person taking action and shall be deemed as unpriced components that are involved in either consumer or producer market transactions.

Air pollution from factories is one example. The cost of air pollution to society is not paid by the shareholders of the factory to the rest of society, but it negatively affects the whole society, as it constitutes anti-social and harmful behavior.

According to Pigou, the existence of externalities is a justification for government intervention. If someone is creating a negative externality, such as the above-mentioned hypothesis of pollution, Pigou supported a tax on such activities to inhibit them.

However, externalities can be positive, and, in that case, Pigou advocated subsidies for activities that created such positive externalities.

These are now called Pigouvian taxes and subsidies, respectively.

4. Definition brought by Longman Dictionary, at feel-good factor | meaning of feel-good factor in Longman Dictionary of Contemporary English | LDOCE (ldoceonline.com), https://www.ldoceonline.com/dictionary/feel-good-factor.

So, the so-called Pigouvian taxes are designed to correct the negative externalities by imposing costs on harmful activities, such as pollution, or rewarding beneficial ones.

Broadly speaking, taxes can have a substantial influence on individuals and businesses. By altering the costs or benefits associated with certain activities, taxes can encourage or discourage specific behaviors in the manners below:

- "Sin Taxes": high taxes on sugary drinks, tobacco and alcohol increase the cost of these products, which can discourage consumption, thereby promoting better dietary choices and reducing the incidence of obesity and related health problems.
- Tax Credits for Education and Retirement Savings: Governments often provide tax credits or deductions for education expenses and contributions to retirement savings accounts. These incentives encourage individuals to save money and invest in their education and their retirement plans.
- Corporate Tax Rates: As seen in the example of TCJA in the U.S., lower corporate tax rates can attract businesses to invest in a particular country or region, influencing decisions on where to locate operations.
- Shifting Consumption Patterns: Sales Taxes may influence consumer behavior by making certain goods and services more expensive. For example, a higher tax rate on luxury goods can discourage excessive spending on non-essential items.
- Taxes on Fossil Fuels: Fuel taxes can lead to reduced consumption of fossil fuels by making driving or using energy-intensive products more expensive, thereby encouraging the use of public transportation, carpooling, or energy-efficient alternatives. In the same manner, governments can incentivize businesses and consumers to reduce their carbon footprint by implementing carbon taxes, which might lead to a more disseminated use of renewable energy sources.

As can be perceived, taxes are not just tools for raising government revenue; they also serve as powerful instruments for modeling behavior across society. By carefully designing tax policies, governments can boost or discourage selected activities, leading to outcomes that align with broader social, economic, and environmental goals.

Note this "alternative use" of taxation may receive some criticism, such as a proper way to calculate it and the fact additional taxes charged over items consumed by the poorest people (e.g., taxation over food and fuel) may hit low-income consumers hardest. Also lobbying may also act favorably or against the sectors that are under this taxation. As published by "The New York Times":[5]

> But the mere fact that Pigovian taxes produce greater benefits than costs doesn't make them an easy sell politically. Like other changes in public policy, a Pigovian tax produces winners and losers. And it's an iron law of politics that prospective

5. Pigovian Taxes May Offer Economic Hope—The New York Times (nytimes.com), https://www.nytimes.com/2013/01/06/business/pigovian-taxes-may-offer-economic-hope.html.

losers lobby harder to block change than prospective winners do for its adoption. That asymmetry creates a powerful status-quo bias that makes even broadly beneficial policy changes hard to achieve.

Despite this punctual criticism, the concept of Pigouvian taxation has a close connection to ESG. And the examples below will bring more light on this.

Even though plastic bags have traditionally been given for free to customers by stores when purchasing goods, since they are a cheap, hygienic and convenient way to carry items, difficulties associated with these items include their environmental impacts—as many of them end up on streets and subsequently pollute major water sources and use of nonrenewable resources for its production, such as crude oil.

Taxation charged over the utilization of plastic bag tax is commonly applicable to restrict the use of these goods at retail establishments, and there has been a global trend towards this type of public price over bags.

Ireland was one of the first countries to introduce a plastic bag tax, known as the Plastic Bag Levy, in 2002. The tax has been highly successful in reducing plastic bag usage by over 90%. Although there was some initial resistance, the public quickly adapted to the levy, with most people choosing to use reusable bags instead of paying for plastic ones, whose cost is EUR 0.22 per bag. The money collected by the payment of this levy finances initiatives to reduce waste and promote the reuse and recycling of goods.[6]

Another remarkable example of taxation aiming to discourage non-sustainable behaviors is the landfill tax, i.e., a fee may be imposed on landfills or other disposal facilities as a means of raising general revenues to generate funds for inspection programs or long-term mitigation of environmental impacts related to disposal, or as a means of inhibiting disposal by raising the cost in comparison to preferable alternatives. Note landfilling is discouraged due to several key reasons:

- GHG Emissions: Organic waste in landfills decomposes anaerobically (without oxygen), and then they produce methane, a potent GHG that contributes substantially to climate change. Also, when waste is buried, the energy and materials dedicated to producing those goods are also lost, which could have been recovered through recycling or composting.
- Limited Land Availability: Many regions are running out of space to locate new landfills. Urbanization and population growth intensify the pressure on available land.
- Resource Inefficiency: Landfilling valuable materials like metals, plastics, and organic matter results in a loss of potentially recyclable or reusable assets. These materials could otherwise be processed and reintroduced into the economy.

6. Plastic bag environmental levy (revenue.ie), https://www.revenue.ie/en/companies-and-charities/plastic-bag-environmental-levy/index.aspx#: ~ :text = Retailers%20who%20supply%20plastic%20bags%20to%20customers%20must,the%20Department%20of%20the%20Environment%2C%20Climate%20and%20Communications.

So, the charge of landfill tax to be paid when disposing waste at a landfill site acts as an obstacle to this destructive practice, being thus considered an example of a "Pigouvian tax," as it means a tax implemented over an activity to inhibit it.

This type of tax is usually charged by weight, and its purpose is to force companies to think about alternative destinations for waste. As a Pigouvian tax, it imposes a financial burden on landfill use, aiming to shift behaviors and attitudes towards the transition to a circular economy.

Not surprisingly, many countries are applying landfill taxation. The U.K.'s landfill tax, introduced in 1996, has significantly reduced the amount of waste sent to landfills and increased recycling rates. The tax has also generated substantial revenue for environmental initiatives. As explained by U.K. Tax Authorities:[7]

> This is a tax on the disposal of material. As such, it encourages efforts to minimise the amount of waste produced and the use of non-landfill waste management options, which might include recycling, composting and recovery.

So, by making landfill disposal more expensive, it encourages waste reduction, recycling, and sustainable design, all of which are key principles of the circular economy. This shift helps move society away from a linear "take-make-dispose" model toward a more sustainable system where materials and resources are continuously cycled back into the economy, reducing the need for raw material extraction and lowering pollution.

These examples show us that taxation, when thoughtfully designed and implemented, can be a powerful tool for driving change across various aspects of society. By using taxes to incentivize or disincentivize specific behaviors, governments can foster environmental sustainability, social equity, responsible corporate governance, and economic development.

For instance, a carbon tax encourages businesses to switch to cleaner energy sources or adopt more energy-efficient technologies.

Just as the Chicken Tax reshaped the automotive industry, other forms of taxation, like Pigouvian taxes, can be utilized to steer consumer behavior and encourage environmental responsibility.

Ultimately, tax policy can be one of the most effective tools for advancing ESG principles and promoting long-term positive changes in society.

7. Excise Notice LFT1: a general guide to Landfill Tax—GOV.UK (www.gov.uk), https://www.gov.uk/government/publications/excise-notice-lft1-a-general-guide-to-landfill-tax/excise-notice-lft1-a-general-guide-to-landfill-tax.

CHAPTER 5

ESG and International Taxation

a OECD AND INTERNATIONAL TAXATION

Companies increasingly need to make deals outside of their home countries. Buying and selling internationally is how they secure their supply chains, expand their customer base, find skilled and unskilled labor force, and supply the population with all goods, services and technology they want.

This is the phenomenon of globalization, and it has intensified tax competition among countries: to attract multinational corporations and investment, some countries offer lower tax rates or favorable regimes, even though it will potentially erode their tax bases.

So, globalization has provided multinational corporations and wealthy individuals with more opportunities to engage in tax avoidance and evasion by exploiting differences in national tax systems and shifting profits to low-tax jurisdictions. Globalization has led to topics like tax base erosion, profit shifting, and tax competition among countries. Digital nomadism idea, for instance, is something recent, and it is linked to this multinational flow of people and businesses.

International Taxation seeks to address these issues through international cooperation and agreements, which aim to combat illegal tax schemes and ensure fair tax competition. Consequently, International Taxation involves the creation of rules and agreements to curb these practices, such as transfer pricing regulations, anti-abuse rules, and information-sharing agreements between tax authorities, although achieving consensus on these issues is often challenging due to differing national interests.

Globalization and international taxation are closely related, as the increased cross-border flow of goods, services, capital, and people has made tax policies more interconnected. These issues have prompted international cooperation through organizations like the OECD that play a central role in shaping international taxation policies and standards.

OECD was founded in 1961 to stimulate economic progress and world trade. It serves as a platform for its 38 member countries to collaborate on economic, social, and environmental policies, providing a global forum to compare policy experiences, seek answers to common problems, identify positive practices, and coordinate domestic and international policies of its members. The OECD also collects and analyzes data to provide insights and recommendations for policymaking.

The organization develops guidelines and best practices on various issues, including taxation, trade, education, and environmental sustainability. For instance, the OECD is responsible for developing and promoting internationally accepted standards for taxation, which serve as a basis for national tax laws and international tax treaties. The OECD Model Tax Convention is a key reference document that helps countries negotiate bilateral tax treaties to prevent double taxation and to allocate taxing rights.

Note double taxation occurs when the same income is taxed by two or more jurisdictions. For example, an individual may be taxed in their country of residence and in the country where the income was earned. To mitigate this, countries often enter double tax treaties normally by following the OECD template that allocates taxing rights and provides mechanisms to avoid or reduce double taxation.

Also, the OECD is developing frameworks like the BEPS Action Plan to ensure that multinational corporations pay their fair share of taxes.

The concept of a "fair share of taxes" refers to the idea that taxpayers should pay an appropriate amount of taxes relative to their income, profits, or wealth. This is based on the principles of equity and fairness, ensuring that those who can pay more contribute proportionately to the Tax Authorities.

The connection between Environmental, Social, and Governance (ESG) principles and the concept of a "fair share" of taxes is increasingly recognized in the corporate world. Companies that adhere to ESG standards are expected to contribute positively to society, which involves paying their fair share of taxes in the jurisdictions where they operate and make wealth.

This social responsibility evidently is part of the "S." Paying fair taxes supports public services and infrastructure, aligning with broader social goals.

Jointly with the crescent international flow of money due to globalization, tax practices are more and more scrutinized by investors, stakeholders, and regulators as part of a company's overall ESG performance. As published by Forbes magazine:[1]

> Increased social interest in tax and government policies and media scrutiny into whether companies are paying a fair amount of tax have led to tax issues becoming an ESG consideration. Businesses are attempting to implement tax policies that demonstrate their ESG commitments as a way to build public and stakeholder trust.
>
> Examples of external pressure for greater transparency around a company's tax position include government officials requesting information on low effective tax rates, analysts asking about tax risk factors described in SEC filings, media outlets

1. Tax as a Component of ESG (forbes.com), https://www.forbes.com/sites/taxnotes/2022/10/20/tax-as-a-component-of-esg/.

accusing multinational companies of underpaying their income taxes, investment funds requiring companies to disclose their global tax policies, and employee whistleblowers providing tax strategy information to tax officials.

While not reflected in the ESG acronym, tax is central to the concept's principles. Carbon taxes on greenhouse gas emissions and green tax incentives encourage sustainable practices.

Tax laws require companies to contribute to the societies in which they operate, which facilitates public trust in responsible corporate actors. Proper tax governance means oversight of an organization's tax strategies and decisions to ensure they align with business objectives and tax reporting. Taxes are critical to the orderly function of a civil society and support the communities in which businesses operate.

Companies that engage in aggressive and/or illegal tax avoidance may face reputational risks and lose the trust of customers and investors who value social responsibility. Also, aggressive tax strategies often involve complex arrangements that may not be sustainable in the long run and the company may be required to pay back large amounts of tax.

Moreover, risky tax strategies often conflict with ESG principles, especially in the "Governance" pillar, which assesses a company's ethics, transparency, and social responsibility. Poor ESG performance can lead to a lower ESG rating, which increasingly affects valuation as institutional investors and ESG-focused funds avoid companies with such low scores. In turn, this reduces access to capital and may lead to a reduction in share price.

Therefore, fair taxation is becoming a critical component of a company's ESG approach, contributing to long-term sustainability and enhancing social equity.

And this is totally connected to how to deal with international taxation, which is a complex field that requires balancing the interests of different countries while ensuring that global economic activities are taxed fairly and efficiently. Some of the most important topics on International Taxation will be presented onwards.

b DIGITAL ECONOMY AND THE FAIR SHARE OF TAXES

The growth of the digital economy and the activities that are performed through technology have been combined with debates about: (i) the types of taxes digital companies should pay; (ii) where to pay them; and (iii) the amount deemed as a fair value of taxation. This increasing part of the global economy comes from new business models based on intangible assets and a lack of physical presence.

Existing taxation mechanisms are based on this traditional economy based on the classic "brick and mortar" presence and consequently impose challenges and complexities—both for governments trying to implement it and for multinational companies—when faced with digital alternatives.

Digital companies may shift profits from high tax countries to subsidiaries in low-tax or no-tax jurisdictions to reduce their overall tax burden. This practice, while legal, raises ethical concerns about whether these companies are contributing their fair share to the countries where they generate significant revenue and where they use the infrastructure paid by tax revenues.

Whether big tech companies are paying their "fair share" of taxes is a complex question that involves legal, economic, and ethical considerations. While these companies habitually operate within the limits of the law, their use of tax avoidance strategies has led to widespread criticism and calls for reform.

Or, as said by "The New York Times" in a 2012 article, properly named "How Apple Sidesteps Billions in Taxes":[2]

> Apple serves as a window on how technology giants have taken advantage of tax codes written for an industrial age and ill suited to today's digital economy. Some profits at companies like Apple, Google, Amazon, Hewlett-Packard and Microsoft derive not from physical goods but from royalties on intellectual property, like the patents on software that makes devices work. Other times, the products themselves are digital, like downloaded songs. It is much easier for businesses with royalties and digital products to move profits to low-tax countries than it is, say, for grocery stores or automakers. A downloaded application, unlike a car, can be sold from anywhere.
>
> The growing digital economy presents a conundrum for lawmakers overseeing corporate taxation: although technology is now one of the nation's largest and most valued industries, many tech companies are among the least taxed, according to government and corporate data. Over the last two years, the 71 technology companies in the Standard & Poor's 500-stock index—including Apple, Google, Yahoo and Dell—reported paying worldwide cash taxes at a rate that, on average, was a third less than other S.& P. companies'. (Cash taxes may include payments for multiple years.).
>
> Even among tech companies, Apple's rates are low. And while the company has remade industries, ignited economic growth and delighted customers, it has also devised corporate strategies that take advantage of gaps in the tax code, according to former executives who helped create those strategies.

Note traditional tax systems are based on the concept of physical presence (nexus) in a country to determine tax liability. However, digital companies can operate in multiple countries without a physical presence, making it difficult to determine where they should be taxed. It adds another complexity to the tax landscape, requiring companies to navigate different tax rules in multiple jurisdictions. This increases compliance costs, markedly for smaller companies that may not have the resources to manage these complications.

For example: a company like Meta (the giant tech company formed by Facebook, Instagram and WhatsApp) can generate significant advertising revenue from users in each country without having "brick and mortar" offices or employees there. Under traditional tax rules, it may not lead to a taxable presence, thus triggering a minimal or no-tax liability in that country.

2. Apple's Tax Strategy Aims at Low-Tax States and Nations—The New York Times (nytimes.com), https://www.nytimes.com/2012/04/29/business/apples-tax-strategy-aims-at-low-tax-states-and-nations.html.

Also, digital economy frequently generates income from intangible assets, such as software, algorithms, and user data, and all of them can be easily transferred across borders.

Then, allocating profits to specific jurisdictions is complicated because the value creation process is dispersed and difficult to attribute. For instance, a company like Google may create technology in one country, store data in another, and earn revenue from users in plenty of countries. Determining how much profit should be taxed in each country is complex and often controversial.

So, ensuring that digital taxation is fair and does not disproportionately affect certain businesses or countries is difficult. There is a risk that digital taxes could either be too lenient, permitting large companies to continue paying low taxes, or too harsh, restraining growth in the digital economy.

As published by CNBC:[3]

> Tech giants have long been criticized for paying little in taxes despite their size. Amazon and other companies have been accused of avoiding taxes by shifting revenue and profits through tax havens or low-tax countries. The companies insist they're doing nothing wrong from a legal standpoint, which is why policymakers are calling for reforms.

One of these reforms is the implementation of digital taxation measures, such as Digital Services Taxes (DSTs), which have been a solution adopted by many countries.

DSTs are also named "GAFA tax," as they refer to taxation mostly targeted to large technology companies, often abbreviated as GAFA (Google, Apple, Facebook, Amazon). These taxes are designed to address the fact these companies produce substantial revenue in many countries but pay relatively little in corporate taxes in those jurisdictions due to the global nature of their operations and profit-shifting strategies above-mentioned.

Therefore, unilateral implementation of digital taxes by individual countries has led to international disputes, particularly with the U.S., where many of the largest digital companies are headquartered.

This has resulted in stressed trade relations and threats of retaliatory tariffs (as seen in the "Chicken Tax" business case), as it can lead to double taxation (as the same income may be taxed by multiple jurisdictions) and can create a heavy burden for companies and discourage investment and innovation. In a 2019 tweet, when this "GAFA Tax" discussion was starting, the then U.S. President Trump said:

> France just put a digital tax on our great American technology companies. If anybody taxes them, it should be their home Country, the USA. We will announce a substantial reciprocal action on Macron's foolishness shortly. I've always said American wine is better than French wine!

His perspective was also influenced by broader concerns about European regulatory actions against U.S. tech giants, as he argued that while the U.S. could regulate its own companies, foreign countries should cease targeting them unfairly.

3. G7 tax deal: Amazon, Google and Facebook respond (cnbc.com), https://www.cnbc.com/2021/06/07/g-7-tax-deal-amazon-google-and-facebook-respond-.html.

This lack of harmonization in how different countries approach digital taxation creates a mixture of rules that can lead to inconsistencies and uncertainty for businesses, and the absence of a unified global approach complicates tax planning and enforcement.

Altogether, it justifies the ongoing efforts by the OECD and G20 to establish a global tax framework that addresses digital taxation. It is not an easy task, as it requires significant coordination and consensus among countries with diverse interests and tax systems. Transitioning to this new framework will be complex and may face resistance from countries benefiting from the current system.

This includes the introduction of a global minimum corporate tax rate and new rules for taxing digital (and other multinational companies) based on where they generate revenue, not just where they are headquartered.

The main idea connected to this objective is Pillar One, which aims to reallocate some taxing rights over multinational enterprises (MNEs) from the countries where they are headquartered to the countries where they have significant consumer-facing activities, regardless of whether they have a physical presence there.

This is a movement from customary tax rules that relied on physical presence (nexus). This initiative reflects the OECD's role in adapting international tax rules to modern economic realities, particularly the challenges posed by digital businesses.

Addressing these challenges requires coordinated global efforts, such as the initiatives by the OECD and G20, to create a fair, efficient, and predictable tax system that reflects the realities of the digital age and the necessity for a fair share of taxes to be paid by digital businesses.

c PROFIT SHIFTING AND BEPS PROJECT

Profit shifting refers to strategies used by multinational corporations to decrease their tax liabilities by moving profits from high tax countries to low-tax or no-tax jurisdictions. This is often done through mechanisms like transfer pricing, where companies set the prices for goods and services sold between their subsidiaries in different countries to shift profits to where they will be taxed less.

Another usual method for shifting profit is for a multinational corporation to use a subsidiary it has in a tax haven to charge costs to the subsidiaries (for management or technical services, for example) it has in other countries and then obtain revenues that will be not taxed or taxed at a low rate.

Another technique is the transfer of intangibles to tax havens, as seen in the previous chapter. In any case, profit or income shifting basically occurs through the pricing of intra-company transactions.

These profits that remain untaxed or undertaxed can trigger a problem for the companies that generate it: the "trapped cash," i.e., profits or earnings that multinational companies hold in foreign subsidiaries and are unable or unwilling to repatriate to their home country due to high tax costs. This often occurs because bringing the money back could raise significant tax liabilities under the home country's tax laws. As a result, the funds remain "trapped" overseas, limiting the company's ability to use them for dividends, investments, or other purposes within its home country.

This issue of trapped cash is so delicate that the 2017 U.S. Tax Reform addressed it by introducing the previously mentioned one-time repatriation tax on the accumulated foreign earnings of U.S. companies. This tax was applied at reduced rates of 15.5% for cash and cash equivalents and 8% for other assets, regardless of whether the earnings were repatriated (instead of the 35% rate, then applied in the country). As also cited, the 2017 tax reform also shifted the U.S. tax system to a territorial one, where foreign profits are generally exempt from U.S. tax, reducing the incentive to keep profits overseas.

A huge amount of money was repatriated to the country because of this regulation (also called TCJA). As shown by the Federal Reserve Bank:[4]

> Balance of payments data show that U.S. firms repatriated $777 billion in 2018, roughly 78 percent of the estimated stock as of end-2017 of offshore cash holdings. Repatriation was strongest in the first half of 2018, when $510 billion was brought back, and continued throughout 2018, albeit at a slower pace.

The size of this inflow of funds back to the U.S. is proof of how relevant the total profits are kept abroad under low-tax jurisdictions. Therefore, profit shifting erodes the tax base of higher-tax countries, leading to reduced tax revenues and increased scrutiny by tax authorities and international organizations like the OECD.

Not surprisingly, OECD is treating this tax erosion through a framework named BEPS, aiming to combat tax avoidance strategies used by multinational corporations by using gaps and mismatches in tax rules to shift profits to low or no-tax jurisdictions. As explained on its website:[5]

> The OECD/G20 Base Erosion and Profit Shifting (BEPS) Project aims to create a single set of consensus-based international tax rules to address BEPS, and hence to protect tax bases while offering increased certainty and predictability to taxpayers.

The BEPS framework includes 15 actions designed to develop transparency, ensure tax fairness, and update international tax rules to address digitalization and other modern economic challenges derived from globalization, as follows:

(1) Address the tax challenges of the digital economy.
(2) Neutralize the effects of hybrid mismatch arrangements.
(3) Strengthen Controlled Foreign Corporation rules.
(4) Limit base erosion via interest deductions and other financial payments.
(5) Counter harmful tax practices more effectively, taking into account transparency and substance.

4. The Fed—U.S. Corporations' Repatriation of Offshore Profits: Evidence from 2018 (federalreserve.gov), https://www.federalreserve.gov/econres/notes/feds-notes/us-corporations-repatriation-of-offshore-profits-20190806.html.
5. Tax Challenges Arising from Digitalisation—Report on Pillar One Blueprint | OECD, https://www.oecd.org/en/publications/tax-challenges-arising-from-digitalisation-report-on-pillar-one-blueprint_beba0634-en.html.

(6) Prevent treaty abuse.
(7) Prevent the artificial avoidance of Permanent Establishment status.
(8) Aligning transfer pricing outcomes with value creation: intangibles.
(9) Aligning transfer pricing outcomes with value creation: risks and capital.
(10) Aligning transfer pricing outcomes with value creation: other high-risk transactions.
(11) Measuring and monitoring BEPS.
(12) Require taxpayers to disclose their aggressive tax planning arrangements.
(13) Reexamine transfer pricing documentation.
(14) Make dispute resolution mechanisms more effective.
(15) Develop a multilateral instrument.

So, all these actions together aim to prevent profit shifting and ensure that taxes are paid where economic activities occur. For the purposes of this book and considering the progress of these debates within the international tax arena, it is important to focus on the first two actions proposed by OECD.

BEPS Pillar One concentrates on addressing the tax challenges taking place from the digitalization of the economy, presented in the previous section. It seeks to ensure that large MNEs, particularly those in the digital and tech sectors, pay taxes in the countries where they have significant consumer-facing activities, even if they do not keep a physical presence there. The message here is that the digital economy cannot be perceived as separate from the rest of the economy.

While Pillar One focuses on reallocating taxing rights to ensure that countries where businesses operate (and not just where they are headquartered) can tax a portion of the profits, Pillar Two focuses on setting a floor on corporate tax rates globally, by establishing a global minimum tax, to reduce the possibility of avoiding taxation through the utilization of low-tax jurisdictions. The purpose of Pillar Two is to make sure that multinational corporations pay a minimum level of tax on profits in every jurisdiction where they function, regardless of where they are headquartered.

Therefore, Pillar Two introduces a minimum effective tax rate of 15% on the profits of large MNEs. This ensures that companies cannot shift profits to low-tax jurisdictions to avoid paying taxes. If a company is paying less than the minimum tax in each jurisdiction, additional taxes can be levied by other countries to bring the rate up to 15%.

By addressing tax avoidance and prompting companies to contribute fairly to the tax systems in the countries where they operate, the BEPS Project supports social equity, a key ESG target. Companies that adhere to BEPS and pay fair taxes are seen as contributing positively to social outcomes, thereby enhancing their social performance under ESG criteria.

d TRANSFER PRICING

Transfer pricing refers to the pricing of goods, services, and intellectual property (IP) exchanged between related entities within a multinational corporation. Since these transactions occur between entities under common ownership, the prices may not reflect market rates, leading to potential tax advantages.

Consequently, transfer pricing rules are designed to ensure that these transactions are conducted at "arm's length," meaning the prices should be like what would be charged between unrelated parties in the open market. This helps prevent profit shifting to low-tax jurisdictions.

Two interesting examples below (Nike and Coca-Cola cases) may illustrate the concept and demonstrate how relevant an adequate governance structure for transfer pricing is.

Nike faced scrutiny over its transfer pricing practices, particularly in Europe, focused on use of intercompany transactions to shift profits from higher-tax jurisdictions to low-tax entities. It was performed specifically by pooling the resulting income in the Netherlands and then using royalty payments to direct that same income forward to other Nike subsidiaries that were not subject to tax at all.

The European Commission investigated whether these arrangements allowed Nike to underreport taxable income in Europe, effectively lowering its tax burden. The case is part of broader efforts by regulators to ensure that multinational corporations pay their fair share of taxes in the regions where they generate significant profits.

On the other side of the ocean, the Coca-Cola transfer pricing case involved a dispute with the U.S. Internal Revenue Service (IRS) over how the company allocated profits between its North American headquarters and foreign affiliates, as the company transferred intangible properties value to subsidiaries in Africa, Europe, and South America between 2007 and 2009.

The IRS adopts the usual definition of transfer pricing, i.e., this pricing should be the same between intercompany transactions that would have occurred if the company completed the transaction with an unrelated party or customer outside the company. According to the IRS website, transfer pricing is defined as follows:

> The regulations under section 482 generally provide that prices charged by one affiliate to another, in an intercompany transaction involving the transfer of goods, services, or intangibles, yield results that are consistent with the results that would have been realized if uncontrolled taxpayers had engaged in the same transaction under the same circumstances.[6]

The IRS argued that Coca-Cola's transfer pricing arrangements undervalued the profits attributed to its U.S. operations, leading to underpayment of taxes in this country. The dispute resulted in a significant tax assessment against Coca-Cola—that may potentially reach USD 9 billion—which the company contested in court. This is the official position of Coca-Cola, published in its quarterly report filed with the Securities & Exchange Commission on July 31, 2024:[7]

6. Transfer pricing | Internal Revenue Service (irs.gov), https://www.irs.gov/businesses/international-businesses/transfer-pricing.
7. Quarterly Filings (10-Q): The Coca-Cola Company (KO), https://investors.coca-colacompany.com/filings-reports/quarterly-filings-10-q.

> On September 17, 2015, the Company received a Statutory Notice of Deficiency ("Notice") from the United States Internal Revenue Service ("IRS") seeking approximately $3.3 billion of additional federal income tax for years 2007 through 2009. In the Notice, the IRS stated its intent to reallocate over $9 billion of income to the U.S. parent company from certain of its foreign affiliates that the U.S. parent company licensed to manufacture, distribute, sell, market and promote its products in certain non-U.S. markets.
>
> The Notice concerned the Company's transfer pricing between its U.S. parent company and certain of its foreign affiliates. IRS rules governing transfer pricing require arm's-length pricing of transactions between related parties such as the Company's U.S. parent and its foreign affiliates. (...)
>
> The Company currently estimates that the payment to be made at that time related to the 2007 through 2009 tax years, which is included in the above estimate of the potential aggregate incremental tax and interest liability, would be approximately $6.0 billion (including interest accrued through June 28, 2024), plus any additional interest accrued through the time of payment. Some or all of this amount, plus accrued interest, would be refunded if the Company were to prevail on appeal.

The case has yet to be resolved but highlights the complexities and risks associated with transfer pricing for multinational corporations.

Further, transfer pricing is closely connected to tax governance as it involves the policies and parameters used by companies to determine the prices for transactions between their subsidiaries across different jurisdictions. And effective tax governance requires that these practices comply with international and local tax laws, ensuring that profits are properly allocated and taxes are paid where economic value is created.

It demands technical analysis and a highly skilled team. Poor transfer pricing practices can lead to tax dodging, erosion of the tax base, and intricated legal disputes (as presented in the examples above), prompting regulatory scrutiny and the need for robust governance frameworks.

Ensuring compliance with transfer pricing goes beyond just avoiding penalties: it is about keeping the integrity of global operations as well as optimizing internal processes, creating opportunities for potential growth in profitability through operational improvements, cost efficiencies and strategic adjustments. Moreover: thorough governance on transfer pricing allows full comprehension by the tax authorities about the business, making things smoother when being challenged.

And a good governance reflects on a tax return named Country-by-Country Reporting, which means a reporting standard usually requires large MNEs (typically applicable to groups with consolidated revenue above a specific threshold, commonly EUR 750 million) to provide a breakdown of their global activities, including revenue, profits, worldwide taxes paid, and other economic activity, on a country-by-country basis. This report is designed to increase transparency in how these groups allocate income and taxes across different jurisdictions.

It is a tool used by tax authorities to assess transfer pricing risks. The information in this report allows them to see discrepancies between where profits are reported and where economic activities occur, highlighting potential transfer pricing issues. By providing this information, it is possible to understand whether a company's transfer pricing practices align with economic activity and value creation in each jurisdiction, helping to detect and prevent profit shifting and tax avoidance.

Another important mechanism that connects proper governance and transfer pricing is the Advanced Pricing Agreement (APA), an arrangement between a taxpayer (usually a MNE) and one or more tax authorities to pre-determine the transfer pricing methodology that will be applied to certain transactions between related parties for a specified period. Its goal is to minimize the uncertainty and risk of transfer pricing disputes between taxpayers and tax authorities.

By agreeing in advance on the transfer pricing method, both parties can avoid costly and time-consuming audits, disputes, and litigation. So, the APA process fosters cooperation and a better working relationship, and it is only achievable when tax governance is working well. And it connects with ESG principles, primarily in the Governance pillar, particularly through the themes of transparency, compliance, and ethical tax practices.

e THE EUROPEAN GREEN DEAL

The European Green Deal is the EU's ambitious strategy to become the world's first climate-neutral continent by 2050, laying out a comprehensive roadmap to achieve sustainability across all sectors.

Released in December 2019 by the European Commission under President Ursula von der Leyen, the Green Deal defines an ambitious roadmap for transforming the EU's economy to achieve sustainability across all sectors while addressing climate change, preserving biodiversity, promoting resource efficiency, and ensuring a just and inclusive transition for all.

It has a robust environmental focus, and it significantly aligns with the "E" (Environmental) component of ESG.

The COVID-19 pandemic, which began shortly after, emphasized the importance of resilience, sustainability, and long-term planning, reinforcing the urgency of achieving these goals. The pandemic emphasized weaknesses in global supply chains, healthcare, and energy systems, which in turn reinforced the argument for a sustainable, green, and digital transformation in Europe.

As a response to the economic fallout from the pandemic, the EU introduced in 2020 the "NextGenerationEU" recovery fund, which allocated EUR 750 billion to support Member States. A sizable portion of these funds (37%) were allocated specifically for green projects associated with the European Green Deal objectives. The plan was to "build back better" by investing in sustainable infrastructure, renewable energy, and green technologies to make the recovery both environmentally sustainable and economically inclusive.

As mentioned, the core objective of the European Green Deal is to achieve net-zero GHG emissions by 2050. This means the EU aims to balance the quantity of GHGs emitted with the amount removed from the atmosphere, in effect eliminating the EU's net contribution to global warming. Aiming to reach this objective, the Green Deal sets an interim target of reducing GHG emissions by at least 55% in 2030 when compared to 1990 levels.

As part of this ambitious plan, the Green Deal aims to decarbonize the EU's energy sector, which is responsible for a large portion of its emissions. This involves expanding the share of renewable energy in the energy mix, leading to more efficiency—with initiatives to improve the energy performance of buildings, support energy-saving technologies, and encourage behavioral changes to reduce energy consumption—and phasing out coal and other fossil fuels.

In this context and recognizing that the transition to a green economy will differently affect diverse regions, industries, and communities, the Green Deal includes a Just Transition Mechanism that provides financial support, amounting to at least EUR 100 billion, to aid regions and workers most affected by the green transition, such as those dependent on coal mining or energy-intensive industries.

Moreover, the Deal aims to create new jobs in sustainable industries, provide reskilling and upskilling opportunities, and protect vulnerable groups to ensure that the transition is socially fair and inclusive. This aligns with the "S" in ESG by leading to a fair and inclusive transition.

Beyond (and from a "S" side of ESG), European transition to a green economy is expected to create new job opportunities in sectors such as renewable energy, sustainable agriculture, circular economy, green construction, and environmental protection, and the Deal encourages research and innovation in green technologies, aiming to position Europe as a global leader in the development and export of sustainable solutions.

The Green Deal pushes industries, such as steel, cement, and chemicals, to implement low-carbon technologies, utilize alternative fuels, and increase resource efficiency. The EU supports innovation and investment in clean industrial processes via financial incentives and regulatory frameworks.

Also, the Green Deal aims to shift to a circular economy, where waste is diminished, resources are reused, recycled, or repaired, and products are designed for durability, reuse, and recyclability. This comprises reducing material use, improving recycling rates, and creating sustainable supply chains.

The Deal supports the transition to sustainable and smart mobility by promoting electric vehicles, investing in public transport, developing high-speed rail networks, and supporting alternative fuels, such as green hydrogen. The initiative also aims to reduce emissions from all modes of transport, including aviation and shipping, by promoting innovation, improving infrastructure, and implementing stricter emissions standards.

The European Green Deal positions the EU as a global leader in climate action by setting ambitious targets and encouraging other countries to increase their climate commitments. The EU aims to promote its standards and practices internationally, including through trade agreements and international cooperation.

Furthermore, the plan promotes green taxation to endorse environmentally friendly behavior and reduce pollution. Environmental taxes are charged on activities that cause environmental harm, such as carbon emissions, waste production, and resource depletion. Also, to accelerate the adoption of green technologies and sustain able business practices, the Green Deal encourages Member States to offer tax incentives for investments in renewable energy, energy efficiency, electric vehicles, and other green technologies.

These incentives could include tax credits, deductions, or accelerated depreciation for environmentally friendly capital expenditures.

Furthermore, one of the foundations of green taxation under the European Green Deal is carbon pricing, including the Emissions Trading System (ETS) and the introduction of a CBAM, which will be shortly commented on in this book.

The ETS puts a price on carbon emissions by setting a cap on the total amount of certain GHGs that can be emitted and allowing companies to buy and trade emission allowances. And the CBAM means a form of carbon border tax, aiming to prevent "carbon leakage," where companies move production to countries with lower climate standards to avoid EU environmental regulations.

The Green Deal involves a range of new regulations, reporting requirements, and standards that companies must comply with, such as the EU Taxonomy for Sustainable Activities and the CSRD, aligned with the governance principles of transparency and accountability in ESG. Additionally, the Green Deal promotes sustainable finance, including the "EU Green Bond Standard" and guidelines for green investments.

The plan encourages companies to align their financial strategies with sustainability goals, ensuring that they are not only profitable but also socially and environmentally responsible.

And the plan—together with the connected tax incentives—confirms how the taxation landscape is changing around the world, thus making crucial the necessity of constant updates for the professionals who manage taxation routines.

CHAPTER 6
Taxpayers, Tax Authorities and Tax Transparency

a TAX GOVERNANCE

Governance is a crucial part of the ESG acronym. While "E" and "S" are rather easy to explain, as both involve concepts everyone can rapidly understand about environmental and social issues, "G" is a little more complex to describe, mainly to those who are not part of the corporate world. Putting simply, governance is the mechanism by which an organization is controlled and operates, including the process of making and enforcing decisions.

Governance is applicable to all relationships a company has, including, for example, labor ones. Labor governance, then, functions as a set of rules, institutions, policies, and practices that regulate the relationship between employers, workers, and governments. It encompasses a wide range of issues related to work and employment, including labor rights, working conditions, wages, benefits, dispute resolution, and occupational safety.

The goal of labor governance is to create a fair, safe, and productive work environment, balancing the interests of workers, employers, and the whole community. And it comprises not only labor legislation but also company's set of policies to make a healthy labor environment (e.g., flexible work arrangements and the offering of professional development opportunities).

Tax governance, in turn, refers to the degree to which taxpayers comply with tax laws and regulations. It includes all the actions and behaviors necessary to fulfill tax obligations, including accurate reporting of income and profits, timely filing and delivery of tax returns, and the payment of any taxes due.

A fair and transparent tax system enhances trust in government and institutions, contributing to SDG 16, which concentrates on peace, justice, and strong institutions. Effective tax collection and administration improve accountability and reduce opportunities for corruption and tax evasion.

Tax compliance is a direct consequence of tax governance, and it is a critical component of any tax system, as it ensures that governments can collect the revenue needed to fund public services and infrastructure. So, the key aspects of tax compliance comprise:

- Timely Submission: Taxpayers are required to file their tax returns by a specified deadline, which varies by jurisdiction and type of taxpayer. Timely filing is a fundamental aspect of tax compliance.
- Accurate Reporting: Taxpayers must precisely report all sources of income, deductions, credits, and other relevant financial information on their tax returns. Misreporting, whether intentional or accidental, can lead to penalties and legal consequences.
- Timely Payment: Taxes owed must be paid by the due date. Delays in payment can result in interest charges, fines, and other penalties.
- Understanding Tax Obligations: Taxpayers are expected to understand and follow the tax laws relevant to their situation, including income tax, corporate tax, property taxes, VAT, and others.
- Use of Legal Tax Strategies: While taxpayers can use legal tax planning strategies to minimize their tax liability, they must avoid illegal activities such as tax evasion or aggressive tax avoidance schemes that violate the essence of the law.
- Documentation: Taxpayers must keep accurate and comprehensive records of all financial transactions, including accounting books, receipts, invoices, and other documentation, to support their tax filings. Proper record-keeping is essential for demonstrating compliance in the event of an audit. It is advisable that documentation comprise a tax strategy and risk tolerance, including how aggressive or conservative it will be in interpreting tax laws.
- Retention Period: Most tax authorities require records to be kept for a certain number of years—the statute of limitation—during which time they may be subject to review or audit.
- Audits and Inquiries: Tax authorities may conduct audits or request additional information to verify the accuracy of a taxpayer's returns. Compliance includes cooperating with these requests and providing the necessary documentation.
- Dispute Resolution: If there is a disagreement between the taxpayer's position and the tax authority, compliance involves following the proper legal channels to resolve the issue, such as administrative and judicial appeals or negotiations.
- Electronic Filing: Many tax authorities offer or require electronic filing of tax returns. Compliance increasingly involves using digital tools to file taxes accurately and on time. So, as tax filings become more digital, taxpayers must also ensure the security of their financial data to prevent fraud and unauthorized access.

Evidently, to properly address all these functions in a duly manner, taxpayers are required to stay permanently updated on tax law changes. Also, a highly skilled team of tax professionals is needed to properly perform and review these routines, as frequent changes in tax laws often make compliance difficult for taxpayers.

Tax compliance is essential for the effective functioning of a tax system and the overall economy. It involves a combination of legal, accounting, financial, and administrative responsibilities that ensure taxpayers meet their obligations under the law.

For some, especially those with straightforward finances and access to good technological tools or professional help, tax compliance can be relatively uncomplicated. For others, particularly businesses or individuals with complex financial situations or who live in jurisdictions with complicated and doubtful tax systems, tax compliance can be more challenging and time-consuming.

In any case, all these challenges, jointly with growing compliance requirements and the demand for tax transparency, mean that companies need to respond in a clear and thoughtful way to a much broader base of stakeholders than before. It includes, of course, government agents, regulators, investors, clients, the media and the public.

Failure to manage tax risks can give rise to reputational, financial, legal and even criminal risks. A tax governance structure helps companies to understand the key tax risks, including the potential focus themes by Tax Authorities, as they have specific rights defined by law to ensure tax systems operate effectively, fairly, and transparently.

Such rights include: (a) assessing and calculating taxes owed by individuals and businesses based on their income, property, and other taxable activities; (b) auditing tax returns, financial records, and other relevant documentation to ensure compliance with tax laws. This includes the right to inspect books, records, and accounts; (c) collecting taxes due, including enforcement measures like seizing assets if necessary; (d) imposing penalties for noncompliance, such as late payment fees, fines for underreporting income, or penalties for fraudulent activities; (e) requesting and accessing information from various sources, including financial institutions, employers, and other government agencies, verifying the accuracy of tax filings; and (f) enforcing tax laws through legal action, including prosecution for tax evasion or other tax-related crimes.

Effective and transparent tax administration is crucial for the functioning of a government, as it provides the necessary revenue to fund public services and infrastructure while maintaining public trust in the fairness and integrity of the tax system.

b TAX TRANSPARENCY AND GRI 207

A key component of strong tax governance is ensuring transparency, which is essential to building trust with stakeholders and promoting ethical business practices.

Transparency is a key element that connects taxation and ESG. It refers to the openness and clarity with which corporations and governments disclose information about their tax affairs and amounts involved. It comprises a range of practices and policies aimed at ensuring that relevant stakeholders—such as tax authorities, press, investors, policymakers, and the public in general—have access to proper, timely, and detailed information about tax-related matters.

Tax transparency is increasingly recognized as an essential component of ESG practices. As organizations face growing scrutiny, their approach to tax matters has become a key indicator of their overall commitment to ethical and sustainable business practices. Overall speaking, here is how tax transparency connects to ESG:

(1) Environmental (E):
  - Funding for Environmental Initiatives: Taxes paid by companies contribute to government revenues that can be used to fund environmental protection and sustainability initiatives. Transparent tax practices ensure that companies are not depriving governments of the resources needed to address environmental challenges.
  - Sustainability Reporting: Increasingly, sustainability reporting frameworks, such as the GRI—to be further commented—include tax transparency as part of their guidelines. This integration stresses the importance of tax transparency in the larger context of corporate sustainability efforts.

(2) Social (S):
  - Fair Contribution to Society: From a social perspective, tax transparency is about a fair contribution to the societies in which a company works. Taxes fund essential public services such as education, healthcare, and infrastructure. By paying their fair share of taxes and being transparent about it, companies display social responsibility and support the well-being of the communities they operate in.
  - Addressing Inequality: Tax transparency can help to reduce economic inequality by ensuring that companies do not utilize loopholes to avoid paying taxes. When large corporations pay their fair share of taxes, governments have more resources to invest in social programs that benefit the whole population, thus reducing inequality.

(3) Governance (G):
  - Ethical Corporate Behavior: Tax transparency is closely tied to the governance prism of ESG. It reflects an organization's commitment to ethical behavior, a well-organized corporate governance, and accountability. It can signal to investors that a company is managing its tax and financial obligations responsibly.
  - Board Oversight and Risk Management: Effective governance includes vigorous oversight of tax strategies by the board of directors. Tax transparency requires that these strategies be clearly articulated, documented, and aligned with the company's overall governance framework. This ensures that tax risks are managed properly and that the company's tax practices do not expose it to reputational or financial risks.

Corporations, especially MNEs, are progressively expected to publicly disclose detailed information about their tax risks and strategies, the amount of tax they pay in different jurisdictions, and how these taxes relate to their overall financial performance. The previously mentioned Country-by-Country Reporting, for example, is a notable initiative related to this topic. This allows tax authorities and the public to see whether profits are being reported and taxed in the locations where economic activities occur. As said by EY Global:[1]

> Absolutely core to this new era of transparency is that information shared with one tax authority will now be rapidly available to all others. This means that the multi-jurisdictional, multiyear impacts of any structure or transaction should be considered more carefully—both moving forward and looking back, because tax authorities will certainly be seeking to use the new data to retrospectively identify and study cases of perceived avoidance from recent years.

In any case, some companies go beyond legal requirements and voluntarily publish tax reports that detail their tax payments, policies, and contributions to public finances. This is often done to demonstrate a commitment to responsible tax practices and to build trust with stakeholders. As published on the KPMG website, for example:[2]

> With environmental, social and governance (ESG) rising on leadership agendas globally, tax practices and governance are becoming critical ESG measures, with tax transparency often being used as a key metric for demonstrating a responsible attitude towards tax. One thing that has become clear, however, is that not all businesses are at the same point in their tax transparency journey and not all have the same tax transparency destination.

Of course, being tax transparent is not an easy task: for businesses, particularly smaller ones, the cost of complying with tax transparency requirements can be significant. Additionally, companies might be concerned that detailed tax disclosures could reveal sensitive and confidential information to competitors or other stakeholders.

In any case, tax transparency is a fundamental aspect of modern tax systems, aiming to ensure that taxes are paid fairly and that the public has confidence in the integrity of corporations in their handling of tax matters. And it has a direct connection with the achievement of the United Nations' SDG, mainly:

- SDG 16—Peace, Justice, and Strong Institutions: Tax transparency supports the achievement of SDG 16, which includes promoting ethical, peaceful, and inclusive societies. Transparent tax practices contribute to robust institutions by ensuring that companies pay their fair share of taxes.
- SDG 17—Partnerships for the Goals: By adopting transparent tax practices, companies contribute to SDG 17, which concentrates on strengthening the

1. Tax transparency and disclosure | EY—Global, https://www.ey.com/en_gl/services/tax-transparency-disclosure.
2. Navigating tax transparency—KPMG Global, https://kpmg.com/xx/en/home/insights/2021/04/navigating-tax-transparency.html.

means of implementation and revitalizing the global partnership for sustainable development. Tax transparency helps build stronger partnerships between governments, businesses, and civil society.

Therefore, tax transparency is a critical attribute of ESG because it links to the three pillars: governance, social responsibility, and environmental impact. By embracing tax transparency, companies not only demonstrate their commitment to ethical and responsible business practices but also contribute to broader societal goals, such as reducing social inequality, funding public goods, and promoting sustainable development.

And to properly divulge it, the most used framework is "GRI 207: Tax 2019." This is a set of standards developed by the GRI to guide organizations in publicly disclosing their tax practices and policies.

It is part of the GRI Standards, which are widely used for sustainability reporting. GRI 207 specifically aims at tax transparency, ensuring that organizations provide comprehensive information on their approach to taxes, tax strategy, governance, and country-by-country reporting. Note that GRI frameworks are focused on the effects of business endeavors in chasing their strategies on the environment and society.

GRI 207 helps organizations show their duty to tax transparency by providing stakeholders with a clear view of their tax practices, including how taxes align with broader business strategies and sustainability goals. Its main components are:

- Public Country-by-Country Reporting: Companies are encouraged to publicly disclose the taxes they pay in each country.
- Tax Governance and Control: Companies must describe their tax strategy and how tax risks are managed.
- Stakeholder Engagement: It encourages companies to communicate how tax issues are managed within the organization.

Also, GRI 207 aligns with global initiatives on tax transparency, such as the previously presented BEPS project, by promoting consistent and comparable tax reporting across different organizations and jurisdictions.

It encourages companies to adopt best practices in tax reporting and transparency, ensuring they meet the expectations of various stakeholders, including investors and regulators, who increasingly demand greater visibility into tax practices and ensuring that tax disclosures are standardized and meaningful.

In addition to these debates directed at private companies, governments are also expected to be transparent about their tax policies, the administration of those policies, and how tax revenues are used.

So, governments should publish detailed, easily accessible budgets that demonstrate how tax revenue is allocated across various sectors, such as healthcare, education, infrastructure, and social welfare. These reports should clearly break down spending by department, project, and region.

A higher level of public services will enable taxpayers to trust the government more. Transparency helps build trust between governments and taxpayers by displaying that tax revenues are being duly applied.

c TAX SHAMING

Cancel culture refers to the phenomenon where individuals, companies, or public figures are boycotted, criticized, or "canceled" by the public or specific groups due to actions or statements that are considered offensive, objectionable, unethical, or unacceptable. This can lead to reputational damage, loss of business, and social ostracism.

It is a controversial phenomenon, and its critique often stems from the perception that it can lead to mob justice and disproportionate punishment. Public figures, celebrities, or even ordinary individuals who are "canceled" may face severe consequences, such as losing their jobs, opportunities, or social standing, sometimes permanently. In any case, social media allows cancel culture to spread rapidly, often without verification of facts. It is worth mentioning too that cancel culture often applies inconsistent standards, where certain individuals or actions are canceled while others are overlooked or ignored.

Tax shaming, in turn, involves publicly criticizing companies for their tax practices, particularly when they are perceived as engaging in aggressive tax avoidance, exploiting loopholes, or not paying their "fair share" of taxes. This criticism often focuses on the ethical consequences of such practices, even if they are legal.

Cancel culture and tax shaming are related in the sense that both involve public backlash and social condemnation, often driven by perceptions of unethical behavior. When these concepts intersect, tax shaming can become a form of cancel culture, where companies are publicly criticized and socially ostracized for their tax practices.

Evidently, this rapid judgment may lead to an undue punishment and an unfair verdict, but cancel culture and tax shaming can surely lead to significant reputational damage. A company that is under shaming because of its tax practices may find its brand harmed, leading to a loss of customer trust and loyalty.

In a BBC 2013 Article,[3] Apple was mentioned as a beneficiary of a tax scheme that allowed its corporate tax rate to be lower than 2%—due to a structure set up in Ireland—while the rate in force in the U.S. at that moment was 35%, and most of its IP was in fact developed therein:

> Apple's tax methods have been unpicked by a US Senate committee that has accused the company of being "among America's largest tax avoiders".
>
> Carl Levin, chairman of the Senate Permanent Subcommittee on Investigations, said Apple, making use of the tax system in the Republic of Ireland, "shifts billions of dollars in profits offshore" that should be subject to US taxes.
>
> He said Apple had a highly developed tax avoidance system through which it had amassed more than $100bn (£66bn) in offshore cash.
>
> The committee said Apple—which Mr Levin called "an American success story"—had created a "complex process" to avoid paying taxes. His committee had earlier said there had been no indication the firm had acted illegally.

3. Apple "among largest tax avoiders in US"—Senate committee—BBC News, https://www.bbc.com/news/business-22600984.

> The firm designated its Irish entities as unlimited companies, which meant it did not have to publish annual accounts. The Senate inquiry has been the first time the structure has been publicly revealed.
>
> The Irish arrangement allowed Apple to pay just 1.9 % tax on its $37bn in overseas profits in 2012, despite the fact average the tax rate in the OECD countries that make up its main markets was 24 % last year.
>
> In a 40-page memorandum, the Senate committee says: "Ireland has essentially functioned as a tax haven for Apple."

Ireland has historically been known for its favorable corporate tax regime, including a low corporate tax rate (traditionally 12.5 %) and specific tax structures that allow multinational companies to minimize their global tax bills. This mechanism of setting up business in Ireland was quite usual, mainly for tech and pharmaceutical, as most of these companies' wealth comes from creative and disruptive ideas, i.e., intangible properties.

Some of the mechanisms associated with Ireland's tax schemes, such as the "Double Irish" structure (described at, "Double Irish With a Dutch Sandwich"—Graphic—NYTimes.com, https://archive.nytimes.com/www.nytimes.com/interactive/2012/04/28/business/Double-Irish-With-A-Dutch-Sandwich.html?_r = 0Reao), have drawn enormous criticism. For example, companies like Amazon, Google, and Starbucks have been condemned in the media[4] and by politicians for routing profits through Ireland to reduce their global tax bills.

Amazon is also largely criticized for not publicly disclosing detailed tax information in every jurisdiction where it operates, making it difficult for investors and the public to assess whether the company is paying its fair share of taxes globally.

Another huge multinational company had been challenged by its tax-aggressive practices. McDonald's came under fire in 2015 when it was revealed that the company had paid almost no corporate taxes in Europe for several years by funneling its European royalties through Luxembourg, where it had negotiated a favorable tax deal. Later, following public pressure and an EU investigation, McDonald's restructured its tax arrangements and began booking more profits in the countries where they were earned. In 2018, McDonald's agreed to pay EUR 1 billion in back taxes to France as part of a settlement.

IKEA, the global furniture retailer, also faced scrutiny over its tax practices, particularly regarding allegations that it engaged in aggressive tax avoidance schemes to reduce its tax liabilities. This scrutiny was intensified after investigations and reports suggested that the company used complex structures to shift profits and reduce its tax burden in various jurisdictions. This scheme included a company named "Inter IKEA," which owned the IKEA brand and managed the IP associated with it, such as trademarks and franchise agreements and another one, "IKEA Group," which ran IKEA stores worldwide, paying royalties to Inter IKEA for the right to use the brand and IP.

4. Google, Amazon, Starbucks: The rise of "tax shaming"—BBC News, https://www.bbc.com/news/magazine-20560359.

These royalties represented a substantial amount of revenue and Inter IKEA (the owner of the IP) was reported to have subsidiaries in Luxembourg and the Netherlands, countries with favorable tax regimes, where royalty payments were transferred, enabling IKEA to pay a low amount of taxes on significant portions of its profits. The investigation held by the European Commission alleged that the structure allowed IKEA to avoid paying nearly EUR 1 billion in taxes between 2009 and 2014.

Public awareness of these practices can lead to significant reputational damage. Customers, investors, and the public may view these companies negatively, leading to pressure to change their tax practices.

So, companies that use tax schemes to significantly reduce their tax liabilities in ways that are seen as ethically questionable or socially irresponsible may be liable to cancelation culture under a tax stamp, the so-called tax shaming. It can be highly detrimental to companies for several reasons, primarily because it affects their reputation, investor confidence, consumer trust, and long-term business prospects. Even if a company's tax strategies are legal, the public perception that they are avoiding paying their "fair share" of taxes can trigger significant criticism.

And the country sometimes referred to as the "Celtic Tiger"—Ireland—was under scrutiny too. Ireland has been historically perceived by some as a tax haven, although the country does not officially identify as one, and its government has taken steps to distance itself from that label. This perception is largely due to Ireland's historically low corporate tax rate and its favorable tax structures, which have attracted many multinational companies, particularly in the technology and pharmaceutical sectors.

The EU has chased high-profile cases against companies using Ireland's tax schemes, such as the Apple case, where the European Commission ordered Apple to pay billions in back taxes to Ireland. As told by the Forbes magazine:[5]

> But now it has actually, finally, happened. No rhetoric, no strong words. Real action. The EU has ordered Apple to pay the Irish government $13 billion in back taxes. The Irish government may not see that money for years as an expensive appeals processes will probably tie up the escrow-held money for the time being. And, more astonishingly, the Irish government doesn't actually want the money: the EU ruled it complicit in giving Apple special tax arrangements.

Pressure from tax shaming can also influence policymakers and regulators. For example, if a company is extensively slammed for its tax practices, it may pressure governments to close loopholes, strengthen tax enforcement, or implement new regulations to ensure a fair and just taxation.

Again, the Irish case is illustrative: the country has generally been viewed as a provider of tax structures that benefited multinational companies. As published by The

5. Apple Falls Victim to Rapidly Changing Public Mood (forbes.com), https://www.forbes.com/sites/jaymcgregor/2016/08/31/apple-falls-victim-to-rapidly-changing-public-mood-around-tax-avoidance/.

New York Times[6] in 2021: "For decades, multinationals moved to Ireland for its low taxes. A new global tax plan has put Dublin on the defensive."

Therefore, in recent years, Ireland has made efforts to reform its tax policies, to align with international standards, and to address concerns related to tax avoidance. While the low corporate tax rate remains, Ireland has moved towards greater tax transparency and cooperation with global tax initiatives. The country has taken steps to align with international tax standards, such as joining the OECD global minimum tax initiative and phasing out controversial tax schemes.

For companies, too, it is time to rethink their tax strategies, as they are increasingly expected to contribute fairly to the societies in which they run their businesses. Using tax schemes to minimize tax payments can be seen as conflicting with broader CSR goals, leading to accusations of hypocrisy and further tax shaming.

Note investors are also paying closer attention to tax practices as part of their assessment of companies' ESG performance. Companies seen as not paying their fair share of taxes may face pressure from socially responsible investors or find themselves excluded from certain investment portfolios.

d A MORE TAX-TRANSPARENT COMPANY FOR A TRAUMATIC REASON: THE VALE CASE

On January 25, 2019, a catastrophe struck Brazil: a tailings dam owned by the mining company Vale—the world's largest iron ore producer, founded in 1942—collapsed near the town of Brumadinho in the state of Minas Gerais, in southeastern Brazil. The dam's failure released a massive wave of mining waste, mud, and debris, causing extensive devastation.

The disaster claimed the lives of at least 270 people (with four still officially missing), and many others were injured or went unaccounted for. The released mud buried Vale's administrative offices, a cafeteria, homes, and farms in its path, causing enormous environmental damage to the Paraopeba River and surrounding areas. The collapse raised serious concerns about mining safety practices and regulatory oversight in Brazil, leading to legal action and calls for improved dam safety standards.

Three years earlier, another dam had failed in Mariana, just 120 kilometers away, killing 19 people and causing an environmental disaster. That dam was jointly owned by Samarco, a joint venture between the mining giants Vale and the Anglo-Australian BHP.

The threat posed by poorly constructed dams in Brazil, especially those near populated areas, extends beyond one company. The repetition of the Mariana tragedy at Brumadinho, with even worse consequences, made it clear that the mining industry had inadequate control over dam safety.

6. Ireland's Days as a Tax Haven May Be Ending, but Not Without a Fight—The New York Times (nytimes.com), https://www.nytimes.com/2021/07/08/business/ireland-minimum-corporate-tax.html.

Vale's global reputation was severely damaged by its ineffective safety practices and environmental negligence. This impacted its relationships with investors, governments, and local communities. Following the tragedy, Vale's CEO and several senior executives resigned amid mounting public and regulatory pressure to demonstrate accountability.

After the disaster, Vale committed to decommissioning all its upstream tailings' dams (similar to the one that collapsed in Brumadinho), as they are considered riskier than other types of dams. This was part of a broader effort to improve dam safety. Vale significantly increased its investment in sustainable practices, aiming to reduce its environmental footprint and improve its social impact. This includes a commitment to decarbonizing its operations and reducing GHG emissions.

In January 2021, Vale reached a settlement agreement with the government of Minas Gerais for approximately BRL 37.7 billion (around USD 7 billion), intended to cover reparations for victims, environmental damage, and economic recovery.

Additionally, Vale pledged to improve transparency around its operations, releasing detailed reports on dam safety, environmental impact, and social responsibilities. The company worked with stakeholders, including regulators and investors, to adopt global best practices for mining and tailings dam management.

These transparency efforts had a tax aspect as well. Vale became the first Brazilian company to disclose a tax transparency report. This action is directly related to the Brumadinho disaster, as indicated in the first paragraph of the comprehensive 56-page report:[7]

> We are publishing this report at a time when we at Vale are writing a new chapter in our history. The consequences of the Dam I rupture at the Córrego do Feijão Mine in January 2019 have reinforced the need to develop and expand a dialogue with our stakeholders in a transparent way. We continue to focus on responsible socioeconomic development in the regions and communities where we operate, and recognize the need to explain how we are delivering against our targets and aspirations.
>
> In 2019, as part of this new chapter, we made a commitment to provide additional information of the taxes we pay in the jurisdictions and locations in which we have a presence, across all our businesses and to all levels of government. (...)
>
> The purpose of this report is to add details and context for an ongoing dialogue with investors, governments, communities and other stakeholders. By doing this, we believe we contribute to a fair, effective and stable tax environment, which helps to create a sustainable society.

Not surprisingly, this first page is entitled as "Message from our CEO," being signed by the executive in this position at that time: Eduardo Bartolomeo. And he literally presents a new mindset of the company by saying that:

> We are on a journey to transform the way we engage with our stakeholders and how we understand each other. We hope these first steps are positive. (...)

7. Available at tax-transparency-report-2019_eng-1 (vale.com), https://www.vale.com/documents/d/guest/tax-transparency-report-2019_eng-1.

> Through our operations, investments and taxes, we make an important contribution to the growth of the global economy. Vale is committed to integrating sustainability into its business by building a strong and positive economic, social and environmental legacy and mitigating the impacts of its operations. The taxes we collect and pay represent one of the ways in which we embrace this responsibility. This report is intended to be concise, understandable and accessible to all of our stakeholders.

At the end of the report, it is said that:

> We continue to manage the consequences of the Brumadinho Dam failure, and support the communities affected by it. The impact goes far beyond financial losses and further information about our activity and remediation plan can be found here. For the purpose of this financial report, we confirm that the costs associated with the event significantly impacted our 2019 year-end results, contributing to an accounting loss for the year. While we reported a loss, we calculated and paid income tax because the expenses arising from the event were, for the most part, recognized as provision.

Another example can be mentioned about a mining company that became more tax transparent after tragedies: for instance, in 2020, Rio Tinto faced global condemnation for the destruction of the Juukan Gorge caves in Australia, a sacred Indigenous site with 46,000 years of history. This incident led to significant reputational damage and calls for better corporate governance.

And in response, Rio Tinto committed to improving its corporate governance, ESG practices, and tax transparency. The company has published detailed tax reports as part of its efforts to rebuild trust with Indigenous communities, investors, and regulators. It continues to align with international tax transparency standards, offering insights into its financial operations and tax contributions worldwide.

Talking specifically about the topic under discussion, the Brumadinho tragedy was caused by the lack of proper governance in dam risk assessment. It resulted in immeasurable environmental and social consequences for the surrounding communities, and the company continues to face scrutiny from courts, regulators, and the public.

Nevertheless, Vale appears more committed to improving ESG (Environmental, Social, and Governance) factors, including a focus on responsible taxation. The tragedy marked a new chapter in the company's tax approach, with detailed reports being published annually since 2019.

What the Rio Tinto and Vale cases teach us is that companies responded to significant tragedies or controversies by increasing their commitment to tax transparency, often as part of broader efforts to improve corporate governance, social responsibility, and environmental impact.

Tax transparency helps these companies in their efforts to rebuild trust with the public, investors, and governments by displaying accountability and a commitment to contributing fairly to the societies in which they operate.

e THE EXTRACTIVE INDUSTRIES TRANSPARENCY INITIATIVE

Several major mining companies, including Vale and Rio Tinto, have committed to advancing tax transparency by aligning with global standards and publishing related reports. Other ones, such as Glencore, BHP Group, Anglo American, Newmont, and South32, are making similar efforts.

This disseminated publication of tax transparency reports is clear evidence of the commitment made by the mining industries to be at the forefront of this movement. And it happens for various reasons, driven by industry's nature, public expectations, and regulatory pressures.

First, mining companies often operate in developing countries and resource-rich regions where the extraction of natural resources plays a vital role in national economies. In these areas, revenues from mining activities are crucial for public finances. However, the wealth generated from mining has someway been historically linked to corruption, environmental degradation, and unequal wealth distribution, contributing to the "resource curse." As a result, mining companies face increasing public scrutiny to ensure they are paying their fair share of taxes and contributing to the well-being of local communities.

Moreover, the mining industry frequently attracts attention due to its environmental and social impacts, such as deforestation, water usage, pollution, accidents, and the displacement of communities. These concerns lead to growing demands for accountability from mining companies, not only regarding their environmental practices but also how they contribute to local and national economies. If a mining company is seen as engaging in tax avoidance or shifting profits to low-tax jurisdictions, it risks significant reputational damage.

In response, tax transparency helps build trust with the public and demonstrates that mining companies are contributing fairly to the development of the countries in which they operate.

To support this, many mining companies align themselves with the Extractive Industries Transparency Initiative (EITI), a global standard that promotes openness and accountability in the management of natural resources. EITI requires companies to disclose taxes, royalties, and other payments they make to governments, while governments must reveal the revenues they receive. The initiative is based on clear principles, which emphasize transparency, accountability, and the responsible management of natural resources.

EITI principles are:[8]

(1) We share a belief that the prudent use of natural resource wealth should be an important engine for sustainable economic growth that contributes to sustainable development and poverty reduction, but if not managed properly, can create negative economic and social impacts.

8. EITI Principles | EITI, https://eiti.org/documents/eiti-principles.

(2) We affirm that management of natural resource wealth for the benefit of a country's citizens is in the domain of sovereign governments to be exercised in the interest of their national development.
(3) We recognize that the benefits of resource extraction occur as revenue streams over many years and can be highly price-dependent.
(4) We recognize that a public understanding of government revenues and expenditures over time could help public debate and inform choice of appropriate and realistic options for sustainable development.
(5) We underline the importance of transparency by governments and companies in the extractive industries and the need to enhance public financial management and accountability.
(6) We recognize that achievement of greater transparency must be set in the context of respect for contracts and laws.
(7) We recognize the enhanced environment for domestic and foreign direct investment (FDI) that financial transparency may bring.
(8) We believe in the principle and practice of accountability by government to all citizens for the stewardship of revenue streams and public expenditure.
(9) We are committed to encouraging high standards of transparency and accountability in public life, in government operations and in business.
(10) We believe that a broadly consistent and workable approach to the disclosure of payments and revenues is required, which is simple to undertake and use.
(11) We believe that disclosure of payments in a given country should involve all extractive industry companies operating in that country.
(12) In seeking solutions, we believe that all stakeholders have important and relevant contributions to make—including governments and their agencies, extractive industry companies, service companies, multilateral organizations, financial organizations, investors and non-governmental organizations.

By adhering to EITI standards, companies strengthen their CSR commitments, ensuring that the profits made from natural resource extraction are shared equitably with the countries and communities where these resources are extracted. The initiative aims to improve governance and reduce corruption in resource-rich countries by encouraging both governments and companies to disclose key financial information related to the extractive industries.

EITI reports offer detailed insights into the payments made by companies and the revenues received by governments, including taxes, royalties, bonuses, and other fees. This level of transparency fosters trust between companies, governments, and local communities, showing that mining companies are not engaging in tax avoidance or aggressive tax practices. Furthermore, EITI empowers civil society organizations to scrutinize how resource revenues are being managed, deterring corruption and mismanagement in the sector.

From a taxation perspective, EITI also helps identify and address issues related to tax avoidance, aggressive tax planning, and illicit financial flows in the extractive industries. By enhancing transparency around company payments and government revenues, EITI contributes to:

- Exposing tax avoidance strategies, such as transfer pricing or profit shifting.
- Encouraging reforms in national tax laws to close loopholes and improve tax compliance.
- Reducing illicit financial flows, often facilitated by opaque financial practices in the sector.

Although some countries may fight to fully implement EITI due to weak governance, political resistance, or lack of capacity, the initiative has grown significantly since its establishment in 2003. Today, over 50 countries have committed to implementing the EITI standard, with support from multinational companies and international financial institutions. Countries that sign up voluntarily commit to adhering to EITI standards and undergo regular "validation" processes to ensure compliance.

In summary, EITI plays a critical role in promoting tax transparency and accountability in the extractive industries. Fostering public disclosure of taxes and other payments helps ensure that revenues from natural resource extraction are properly managed, contribute to sustainable development, and are not lost to corruption or tax avoidance.

By fostering improved tax governance and public trust, EITI ensures natural resource wealth is managed transparently and fairly.

CHAPTER 7

Carbon Credits and Its Tax Effects

a CARBON CREDITS MECHANISM

The Paris Agreement is a landmark international treaty on climate change, adopted at the 21st Conference of the Parties in Paris, France, in December 2015. It is highly relevant because it represents an unprecedented global consensus (with 195 countries signing and 190 ratifying) and provides a robust platform for ongoing international cooperation on climate issues and on the necessity to address climate change and sets out an agenda for collective action to limit global warming and mitigate its impacts.

The Paris Agreement aims to limit global warming to well below 2°C (3.6°F) above preindustrial levels and to make efforts to limit the temperature increase to 1.5°C (2.7°F). This goal is based on scientific evidence showing that exceeding these thresholds could lead to critical and irreversible effects on ecosystems, human health, food security, and global economies.

Establishing a clear temperature target provides a concrete objective for international climate efforts. It signals the urgent need to reduce GHG emissions globally and serves as a benchmark to measure the progress and success of climate actions.

Even though the beginning of the carbon (CO_2) market can be traced back to the 1997 Kyoto Protocol, Article 6 of the Paris Agreement explicitly recognizes the role of carbon markets in helping countries meet their climate targets, known as NDCs. It provides a basis for voluntary cooperation between countries to accomplish emission reduction goals.

Also, under Article 6, participating countries must follow transparent reporting and accounting practices to ensure that their carbon credit transactions are accurately reflected in their climate action plans and contribute to the overall reduction of global GHG emissions. This is critical for maintaining the integrity of the carbon market and ensuring that global emissions are genuinely reduced.

This agreement, through its support for market mechanisms, encourages the involvement of private sector entities in carbon trading. Businesses can participate in both compliance (regulated) markets and voluntary carbon markets, contributing to emissions reductions through investments in carbon credit projects.

Thus, the 2015 Paris Agreement is a pivotal tool for galvanizing global efforts to combat climate change, providing a framework for reducing emissions, building resilience, mobilizing finance, and fostering international cooperation toward a more sustainable future. Overall, the Paris Agreement establishes the necessary rules and guidelines to facilitate the use of carbon credits in both compliance and voluntary markets, making them crucial in the global effort to combat climate change.

But the question is: What is a carbon credit?

A carbon credit is a tradable permit or certificate that represents the right to emit one ton of CO_2 or an equivalent amount of another GHG, such as methane (CH_4) or nitrous oxide (N_2O). So, carbon markets turn CO_2 emissions into a tradable permit, a commodity, by giving it a price.

Carbon credits are a key component of market-based policies to reduce global GHG emissions and alleviate climate change, and their primary purpose is to provide an economic incentive for companies, organizations, or individuals to reduce their GHG emissions. They do this by allowing entities that reduce their emissions below a certain level to sell credits to those that exceed their emission targets.

When an entity acquires a carbon credit, it is essentially compensating for one ton of its own CO_2 emissions by ensuring that an equivalent amount of CO_2 is reduced or removed elsewhere. This is known as "offsetting" emissions. To count as an offset, a carbon credit must be "withdrew" meaning it is taken out of circulation and cannot be sold or used again. This ensures that the offset is permanent and avoids double counting of emissions reductions.

Therefore, companies can decide to reduce emissions internally or purchase credits from external projects that offer more cost-effective reductions. And carbon credits provide a flexible, cost-effective way for organizations to meet emissions reduction targets. And there are two main types:

(1) Regulated market credits: These are used in mandatory, government-regulated carbon markets (like the European Union Emissions Trading System, EU ETS). Companies are required to hold a specified number of credits to cover their emissions, and they can buy or sell these credits depending on whether they emit more or less than their allowed amount. In these regulated markets, a government sector sets a cap on the total amount of GHGs that can be released by covered entities. Companies are given or must buy a certain number of carbon credits, which they can trade among themselves based on their emission levels.

(2) Voluntary credits: These are traded in voluntary carbon markets by organizations looking to offset their emissions for sustainability goals or CSR aims. Voluntary credits often come from projects that reduce, avoid, or remove carbon from the atmosphere.

In any case, carbon credits are typically generated through projects that reduce emissions or remove carbon from the atmosphere. Common project types include:

- Renewable Energy Projects: Wind, biomass, solar, and hydroelectric projects that replace fossil fuel-based energy generation. Thus, the project developer can receive carbon credits to avoid emissions using renewable energy instead of fossil fuels.
- Forestry and Land-Use Projects: As forests work as natural carbon sinks, removing CO_2 from the atmosphere and storing it in trees, soil, and other biomass will absorb CO_2 from the atmosphere.
- Methane Capture Projects: Capturing methane emissions from landfills, agriculture, or waste treatment and converting it into energy. For example, anaerobic digesters capture methane emissions from agricultural waste and convert them into biogas for energy use.
- Energy Efficiency Projects: Upgrading buildings, factories, or transportation systems to reduce energy consumption and emissions. For example, buildings require energy for space heating and cooling, water heating, lighting, cooking, and appliances and turning their rooftops into solar farms may generate these credits.

Evidently, these project models, the expected scenarios, their background and the effective register must be validated by an accredited third-party auditor. This validation involves assessing the project documentation, including the emissions reduction methodology, project feasibility, and potential environmental or social impacts.

Also, the carbon market is one of the most potent tools for facing climate change and a powerful technique to be adopted in the business sustainability strategy. Constant refinement and data tracking are decisive to its success.

Note that carbon credits are appealing to companies because they are often cheaper than other mitigation projects, and their purchase does not require a change in the company's operations or supply chain.

However, firms should carefully consider purchasing carbon credits because, as a newborn industry, a lot of challenges and criticism are taking place.

b CHALLENGES AND CRITICISM

Companies worldwide are more and more committing to achieving net-zero carbon emissions, sometimes through a regulatory push and sometimes voluntarily. Carbon credits are a crucial tool for this net-zero journey by allowing companies to offset emissions they cannot yet cut. Consequently, the carbon credit market is expected to grow substantially in the coming years.

However, as a worthwhile element in the fight against climate change, its utilization faces several challenges and criticisms. These concerns revolve around the effectiveness, integrity, and implementation of carbon credit systems, as follows:

- Questionable Additionality: For a carbon credit to be legitimate, the emission reduction must be "additional"—meaning it would not have occurred without the project funded by the carbon credit. Nevertheless, many projects fail to prove additionality, and some might have happened regardless of the carbon credit revenue, so this raises skepticism about whether the credits represent real emissions reductions.

- Baseline Manipulation: The baseline scenario (what emissions would have been without the project) can at times be exaggerated, making the project's emission reductions seem more significant than they in fact are. Overestimated baselines can result in issuing more credits than the genuine reductions reached.
- Short-Term Solutions: Some projects, like certain reforestation efforts, may propose only temporary carbon sequestration. For example, if trees are cut down, burned, or lost to pests or diseases in the future, the carbon they collect could be released back into the atmosphere.
- Risk of Double Counting: Double counting occurs when the same emissions reduction is claimed by multiple parties—for example, both by the country where the project is located and by the company buying the carbon credit. This undermines the integrity of carbon markets and can lead to an overestimation of global emissions reductions. It can occur in various forms, including double issuance, double claiming, and double use, that involve using the same carbon credit more than once. For example, if a credit is sold to multiple buyers or if a single credit is retired by one entity but also resold to another.
- Weak Accounting Frameworks: As it is still an emerging market, lack of standardized and robust accounting frameworks and registries can make it difficult to track carbon credits accurately and avoid the above-mentioned double counting. So, if carbon credits are perceived as unreliable or untrustworthy, the overall effectiveness of carbon markets as a climate tool may be considered suspicious.
- Land Rights and Displacement: Some forestry or land-use projects aimed at generating carbon credits have led to conflicts over land rights, with local communities or indigenous peoples being displaced or having limited access to their traditional lands.

A recent episode in Brazil illustrates this warning on land's legal property, as "Brazil's environment minister has urged greater caution from international buyers of carbon credits after police in the South American country uncovered allegedly fraudulent emissions-offset schemes on stolen land in the Amazon. Marina Silva said recent revelations about criminal enterprises suspected to have illegally sold millions of dollars of carbon certificates from the world's largest rainforest were a 'serious problem' that could harm the reputation of a tool supporters say helps fight global warming":[1]

- High Administrative and Verification Costs: The process of developing, verifying, certifying, and monitoring carbon credit projects can be complex and

1. Brazil minister warns carbon credit buyers to beware fraud (ft.com), https://www.ft.com/content/ea246444-7bd4-4d1f-8bf0-8adcd3a7eba4.

costly, especially for smaller projects. These costs can reduce the overall financial viability and effectiveness of carbon credit schemes.
- Misleading Marketing: Some corporations announce themselves as being "carbon neutral" without providing full transparency about their actual emissions or reduction efforts, leading to greenwashing.
- Variable Quality of Credits: Not all carbon credits are of equal quality. Credits from projects with inadequate audit standards or questionable environmental impact may not provide real or long-lasting emissions reductions. This can ruin trust in the entire carbon credit market.

Connected to this specific topic, the Guardian published an article accusing Verra—the world's leading certifier of carbon credits—of grossly exaggerating the emissions reductions linked with its "avoided deforestation" credits:[2]

> The forest carbon offsets approved by the world's leading certifier and used by Disney, Shell, Gucci and other big corporations are largely worthless and could make global heating worse, according to a new investigation.
>
> The research into Verra, the world's leading carbon standard for the rapidly growing \$2bn (£1.6bn) voluntary offsets market, has found that, based on analysis of a significant percentage of the projects, more than 90% of their rainforest offset credits—among the most used by companies—are likely to be "phantom credits" and do not represent genuine carbon reductions.
>
> The analysis raises questions over the credits bought by a number of internationally renowned companies—some of them have labelled their products "carbon neutral", or have told their consumers they can fly, buy new clothes or eat certain foods without making the climate crisis worse.
>
> But doubts have been raised repeatedly over whether they are really effective.

Verra strongly disagreed with the conclusions of The Guardian by explaining that the metrics of measurement used by the scientists behind the study do not effectively understand the reality on the ground.

In any case, harm was done.

As can be perceived, carbon credits face significant challenges related to ensuring environmental integrity, avoiding greenwashing, addressing social and equity concerns, and providing long-term, systemic solutions to climate change.

While they offer a flexible mechanism for reducing emissions and promoting sustainable development, they must be carefully managed and continuously improved to address these criticisms and maximize their effectiveness in combating climate change.

And how to fix these imperfections in a nascent market is the topic to be discussed in the next chapter.

2. Revealed: more than 90% of rainforest carbon offsets by biggest certifier are worthless, analysis shows | Carbon offsetting | The Guardian, https://www.theguardian.com/environment/2023/jan/18/revealed-forest-carbon-offsets-biggest-provider-worthless-verra-aoe.

c COMPLIANCE AND REPORTING

Despite these challenges, there are strategies and frameworks in place to enhance the credibility and effectiveness of carbon markets.

New challenges produce new markets, and the current climate change crisis is no exception. Voluntary carbon market is a real example, and there are plenty of companies paying someone else to either reduce their emissions or capture their carbon to compensate for their environmental footprint and even use carbon credits to get to carbon-neutral status. The French oil giant company Total Energies is an example, and Bloomberg announced on August 30, 2024, that:[3]

> French oil major TotalEnergies SE signed a $100 million deal to curb its greenhouse gas emissions by buying carbon credits generated by forest-protection projects across the US.
>
> The agreement was signed with climate-solution adviser Anew Climate and US forest landowner Aurora Sustainable Lands, who will provide operational oversight, according to a statement on Friday. TotalEnergies will use the credits generated to cancel emissions after 2030.
>
> TotalEnergies has said it plans to invest $100 million a year to build a portfolio of projects capable of generating at least 5 million tons of carbon credits per year by 2030.

The carbon credits market is indeed alive, and it is here to stay. And—as a nascent industry—it is necessary to fix its previously mentioned imperfections, and its future will depend on several factors, including regulatory developments, market integrity, technological advancements, and global climate policy commitments.

In addition, investors, consumers, and other stakeholders are pressuring companies to demonstrate meaningful climate action. Participation in carbon credit markets can help companies show tangible efforts toward reducing their climate impact, especially for sectors where direct emissions reductions are challenging.

As presented by McKinsey consulting firm:[4]

> More and more companies are pledging to help stop climate change by reducing their own greenhouse-gas emissions as much as they can. Yet many businesses find they cannot fully eliminate their emissions, or even lessen them as quickly as they might like. The challenge is especially tough for organizations that aim to achieve net-zero emissions, which means removing as much greenhouse gas from the air as they put into it. For many, it will be necessary to use carbon credits to offset emissions they can't get rid of by other means.

Therefore, a growing number of companies are making net-zero commitments to reduce their carbon footprint. For most of these companies, carbon credits offer a way

3. TotalEnergies Invests USD 100 Million in U.S. Forests for C02 Credits—Bloomberg, https://www.bloomberg.com/news/articles/2024-08-30/totalenergies-invests-100-million-in-us-forests-for-c02-credits.
4. Carbon credits: Scaling voluntary markets | McKinsey, https://www.mckinsey.com/capabilities/sustainability/our-insights/a-blueprint-for-scaling-voluntary-carbon-markets-to-meet-the-climate-challenge.

to offset emissions that are currently difficult or costly to eliminate through direct reductions.

So, the increasing emphasis on corporate sustainability and climate responsibility is driving this demand for accredited carbon credits. And here are some key strategies and approaches to improve its reliability and to ensure they genuinely contribute to reducing global GHG emissions:

- Elaborate Robust Methodologies: carbon credit measures should adopt accurate, scientifically based methodologies to calculate emissions reductions, aiming to ensure these parameters are real. Consequently, independent third-party verification should be obligatory for all carbon credit projects. Auditors must be accredited, highly skilled and consistently reviewed to ensure impartiality, expertise, and reliability.
- Similarly, long-term monitoring and reporting for projects is advisable, especially those involving carbon sequestration in forests or soils. This ensures that carbon continues to be stored for the expected period and that any reversals are rapidly identified and accounted for.
- Develop a central register that properly tracks the lifecycle of every carbon credit, from issuance to retirement. These registries should be publicly accessible and allow stakeholders to verify the source, ownership, and status of each credit. It will trigger a desirable unique Identification for Credits to avoid double counting, double issuance, or double use. This unique ID would allow for unified tracking and monitoring across different standards and jurisdictions.

  Additionally, it may use blockchain technology to create a transparent, tamper-proof record of carbon credits. Blockchain can enhance traceability, reduce administrative costs, and ensure that credits are not counted or used multiple times.
- In the same way, the set-up of clear, standardized international rules for carbon credit accounting and trading under international frameworks like the Paris Agreement (particularly Article 6). This includes defining "corresponding adjustments" to avoid double counting and setting guidelines for transparency and environmental integrity.
- These international rules would promote Transparency and Consumer Awareness by encouraging companies and organizations to be transparent about their utilization of carbon credits, including the types of projects supported, the credit standards used, and the specific climate benefits to be achieved. This helps consumers and stakeholders make informed choices and reduces the risk of greenwashing.
- Also, it may give support and capacity building for developing countries to participate effectively in carbon markets, ensuring that they have the tools, resources, and governance structures needed to develop high-quality and trustable carbon credit projects that will deliver real benefits to local communities, including fair compensation, respect for land rights, and involvement in decision-making processes.

- Moreover, it is recommended to introduce and enforce penalties for organizations or projects that fail to comply with carbon credit standards or engage in fraudulent activities. This creates a deterrent against malpractice and incentivizes compliance.

So, by addressing the regulatory, fiscal, legal and standardization difficulties and challenges—and creating long-term demand incentives—the supply of high-quality carbon credits needed to meet the targets of the global climate will be efficient and trustable. Again, McKinsey's report brilliantly addresses this topic by stating:

> Today's voluntary carbon market lacks the liquidity necessary for efficient trading, in part because carbon credits are highly heterogeneous. Each credit has attributes associated with the underlying project, such as the type of project or the region where it was carried out. These attributes affect the price of the credit, because buyers value additional attributes differently. Overall, the inconsistency among credits means that matching an individual buyer with a corresponding supplier is a time-consuming, inefficient process transacted over the counter.
>
> The matching of buyers and suppliers would be more efficient if all credits could be described through common features. The first set of features has to do with quality. Quality criteria, set out in "core carbon principles," would provide a basis for verifying that carbon credits represent genuine emissions reductions. The second set of features would cover the additional attributes of the carbon credit. Standardizing those attributes in a common taxonomy would help sellers to market credits and buyers to find credits that meet their needs.

By improving standards, enhancing transparency, and integrating carbon credits into broader climate strategies, carbon markets can play a vital role in achieving global climate goals and fostering innovation in emissions reduction technologies.

As a highly positive example, in September 2020, climate scientists from The University of Oxford, the U.K., released a guide on carbon offsetting, the Oxford Principles for Net-Zero Aligned Carbon Offsetting.[5,6] These are highly relevant because they provide a comprehensive framework to ensure that carbon offsetting contributes meaningfully to global climate goals, particularly the goal of achieving net-zero emissions by mid-century.

These principles are designed to address many of the challenges and criticisms associated with carbon offsetting, offering guidance on how offsets can be used responsibly and effectively:

- Principle 1: Reduce emissions, use certified offsets, and use best practices for offsetting strategies.
- Principle 2: Remove more carbon from the atmosphere than is currently being emitted.
- Principle 3: Carbon needs to be locked away indefinitely.
- Principle 4: Industry standards to create net zero-aligned carbon offsetting.

5. Oxford launches new principles for credible carbon offsetting | University of Oxford, https://www.ox.ac.uk/news/2020-09-29-oxford-launches-new-principles-credible-carbon-offsetting.
6. University of Oxford, "The Oxford Offsetting Principles," https://www.smithschool.ox.ac.uk/research/oxford-offsetting-principles, accessed September 2024.

Regulation of the carbon markets is essential, and industries should establish alliances to ensure agreements are adhered to as they develop over time in accordance with best practices. And how to tax these credits is part of these new world strategies and regulations.

d TAXATION OF CARBON CREDITS

The taxation of sales and purchases of carbon credits depends on several factors, including the country or jurisdiction, their type, the purpose of the transaction, and the tax status of the parties involved. However, there are some common principles and approaches to how these transactions are typically taxed on their sales:

- Corporate Income Tax: When a company sells carbon credits, the revenues from the sale are generally considered taxable income. So, it is added to the company's gross income (revenue less expenses and costs) and taxed according to the applicable corporate income tax rates in the jurisdiction where the company is based.
- Capital Gains Tax: In some jurisdictions, if carbon credits are accrued as a capital asset (e.g., an investment or held for longer-term use), the sale might be liable to capital gains tax. The tax rate may vary based on whether the carbon credits were held for a short-term or long-term period, and the gain is normally considered the difference between the sale price and the acquisition cost of the credits.
- VAT or Goods and Services Tax (GST): In some countries, the sale of carbon credits is also subject to VAT or GST, which is typically charged at the standard rate applicable to the seller. The buyer, if also registered as a VAT or GST taxpayer, may be able to reclaim the VAT or GST paid as a tax credit.
- Sales Tax: In jurisdictions that do not have VAT or GST, a sales tax may apply to the sale of carbon credits. The application of sales tax will depend on local laws and whether carbon credits are classified as taxable goods or services.

However, the purchase of carbon credits is usually liable to the following tax considerations:

- Deductibility for Buyers: The cost of purchasing carbon credits may be tax-deductible for companies if they are acquired for legitimate business purposes, such as complying with regulatory obligations or achieving voluntary carbon neutrality. Generally, this deduction is allowed in the year the credits are used or retired.
- Treatment as Inventory or Capital Asset: Depending on the purpose of the purchase, carbon credit may be classified as inventory (if it is bought for resale) or as a capital asset (if held as part of an investment strategy). This classification influences how the credits are recorded on the balance sheet and the timing of any associated tax deductions or liabilities.

For entities that generate carbon credits by implementing their own "green" projects (such as reforestation, renewable energy, or energy efficiency projects), the income from selling these credits is generally subject to taxation, as previously stated. This income is often considered part of the business's gross revenue and taxed accordingly. And in some jurisdictions, projects that generate carbon credits may be eligible for specific tax incentives, such as tax deductions, exemptions, or credits, especially if the projects contribute to environmental goals or sustainable development.

When this transaction is made between parties located in different countries, the tax treatment may be influenced by double taxation agreements between countries. These agreements can help determine which country has the taxing rights and how foreign taxes paid are credited or deducted. Also, transfer pricing rules may apply for multinational companies trading carbon credits within their group entities in different countries. So, companies must ensure that transactions are conducted at arm's length and documentation is maintained to comply with local tax regulations.

In any case, both buyers and sellers must maintain accurate and proper records of carbon credit transactions, including purchase and sale agreements, invoices, valuation methods, and the purpose of the transaction. This adequate documentation is needed to comply with local tax laws and to support any deductions, exemptions, or claims made on tax returns.

In addition, some jurisdictions require transparency in reporting carbon credit transactions, and companies may be subject to audits to ensure compliance with tax regulations. Failure to properly account for and report these transactions can lead to penalties or fines.

As another important topic, tax incentives for the sale of carbon credits can vary significantly depending on the country, the type of carbon credits involved, and the specific policies in place. In some jurisdictions, income derived from the sale of carbon credits may be partially or fully exempt from income tax.

For example, in Australia, certain types of carbon credits, such as those generated from eligible reforestation or land-use projects, may be qualified for concessional tax treatments. The income from selling these credits might be tax-exempt or subject to lower rates.

And there is a reduced capital gain tax rates in the U.S. and Canada, as well as colossal incentives in these North American countries for initiatives connected to air capture technologies, as described by Forbes magazine:[7]

> In the fight against climate change, direct air capture technologies have emerged as a crucial component of global strategies to reduce atmospheric CO2 levels. Both the United States and Canada have recognized the importance of supporting these technologies through financial incentives. The U.S. Inflation Reduction Act and Canada's Carbon Capture, Utilization, and Storage Investment Tax Credit are two

7. How U.S. and Canadian Government Direct Air Capture Incentives Compare (forbes.com), https://www.ox.ac.uk/news/2020-09-29-oxford-launches-new-principles-credible-carbon-offsetting.

> major initiatives aimed at accelerating the adoption of carbon removal technologies. Both countries have the natural resources and subsurface storage capacity to become global leaders in the emerging carbon removal industry, offering not only a climate opportunity, but an economic opportunity as well.
>
> In June, Canada passed its monumental CCUS ITC legislation as part of Bill C-59, signaling support for emerging carbon capture technologies. The CCUS ITC is a refundable tax credit that applies to eligible expenditures incurred for qualified carbon removal projects that capture, transport, store, or use carbon dioxide (CO2) that would otherwise be released into the atmosphere. Administered by the Canada Revenue Agency and Natural Resources Canada, it's a giant leap forward for green tech innovation in Canada and presents a promising economic avenue for the nation.
>
> While monumental, Canada's CCUS ITC follows a similar law as that of its southern neighbor. The U.S. passed the Inflation Reduction Act in 2022, which focuses on reducing greenhouse gas emissions and promoting clean energy initiatives, among other important elements. Both meant as tax incentives, the IRA has already enhanced or created 20 tax incentives for clean energy and manufacturing, including the 45Q production tax credit, a credit of up to $130 per tonne of CO2 captured using direct air capture technologies.

Also, EU countries may offer incentives under the EU ETS for companies to invest in low-carbon technologies and practices, including favorable tax treatment for projects that help meet national carbon reduction targets. By the way, European efforts will be commented on in the next chapter.

In any event, as this is a new matter and it is still under discussion, it is important for corporations to discuss with tax professionals and to stay informed about the specific tax rules and regulations in their respective regions to ensure compliance and optimize their tax position.

With increasing regulation and taxation of carbon emissions, companies need to address greater compliance risks. ESG frameworks accentuate risk management, including regulatory obedience and compliance. Companies that proactively manage their carbon liabilities by reducing emissions and purchasing carbon credits (and adequately taxing it when selling) are better positioned to handle these risks and demonstrate strong governance.

e CARBON BORDER ADJUSTMENT MECHANISM

The CBAM is a policy tool proposed by the EU to address carbon leakage, i.e., the action that occurs when companies transfer their production to countries with less severe climate policies or regulations, thus leading to an increase in carbon emissions in those countries. It is also denominated as "carbon leakage."

This movement is caused by climate policy asymmetries among countries, usually when one country determines, ahead of others, to apply ambitious policies to boost industries to transition to carbon-neutral production, and these policies may cause producers to seek another spot to implement their factories.

Therefore, CBAM is designed to level the playing field between domestic producers in countries with rigorous carbon pricing (like the EU) and foreign producers in countries with ineffective or no carbon pricing.

The European Commission adopted a proposal for this mechanism in July 2021 as part of the EU's "Fit for 55" strategy package, that aims to cut GHG emissions by at least 55% by 2030 when compared to 1990 levels and to accomplish climate neutrality by 2050. As explained by the Center for Strategic and International Studies (CSIS):[8]

> For Europe, the CBAM is a critical component of their climate plan. As the European Union ramps up its efforts to reduce emissions with its cap-and-trade system, the border adjustment is meant to prevent emitters from packing up and leaving the European Union, and avoiding the tightening regulation while maintaining market access through trade. The move reaffirms the European Union's sense of climate leadership as policymakers there can also say that this is a way to incentivize foreign producers to produce more cleanly.

A typical carbon tax is a fee imposed on fossil fuels, such as coal, oil, and natural gas, which are major sources of GHG emissions, so this tax is usually applied to make it more expensive to use fossil fuels. So, by putting a price on carbon, it creates a financial incentive for companies and individuals to reduce their carbon footprint and invest in cleaner energy sources. CBAM goes beyond a regular carbon tax, as it works as a transnational one, being charged over EU companies for the emissions embedded in the goods they import.

CBAM is first levied on imports of carbon-intensive goods like cement, iron and steel, aluminum, fertilizers, and electricity. These sectors were initially selected because they are at high risk of carbon leakage. Through the imposition of a carbon price on imports, CBAM discourages companies from relocating their production to countries with lower environmental standards.

Importers of covered goods into the EU are needed to acquire CBAM certificates, which relate to the carbon emissions embedded in the imported goods. The price of these certificates reflects the weekly average auction price of EU ETS allowances.

If the exporting country already has a carbon pricing mechanism in place, the cost paid for carbon in that country is deducted from the CBAM charges. This prevents double-charging and promotes global carbon pricing harmonization.

CBAM will be phased in gradually and its full application, including financial obligations, is planned to begin in 2026. Revenue from CBAM certificates will be used to fund the EU's climate and energy objectives, including the capital needed for green technology and supporting the transition to a low-carbon economy, as well as possibly providing financial assistance to developing countries to adopt greener practices.

Also, CBAM implementation can stimulate innovation and investment in green technologies, as companies will seek to reduce emissions to remain competitive in the EU market. This may accelerate the development and adoption of cleaner production processes, renewable energy sources, and energy-efficient technologies.

---

8. The United States Should Learn to Live with EU CBAM (csis.org), https://www.csis.org/analysis/united-states-should-learn-live-eu-cbam.

An important topic to be commented on herein is that CBAM affects international commerce in several ways, and it can lead to conflicts with trading partners who view it as a trade obstruction or protectionist measure. Then, some countries may challenge CBAM through the World Trade Organization (WTO), arguing that it discriminates against their exports in an unfair way. To mitigate this, the EU designed CBAM to align with WTO rules by ensuring it is nondiscriminatory and reflects the actual carbon content of products.

Observe that under Article XX of the General Agreement on Tariffs and Trade, WTO members can justify trade measures if they are required to shield human, animal, or plant life or conserve exhaustible natural resources. This is exactly the rationale used by the EU, arguing that CBAM is an environmental measure aimed at combating climate change, which could potentially qualify it for this exception.

However, critics argue that CBAM could disadvantage foreign producers who are unable to meet the same carbon costs as EU producers, being unfair to developing countries that may not have the same resources or capacity to implement robust carbon pricing mechanisms. It could limit their market access to the EU, potentially harming their economies.

In this context, the above-mentioned study published on the CSIS website states that:

> It should be no surprise that the biggest exporters of carbon-intensive goods into the European Union are up in arms. The BRIC countries have called it discriminatory, unilateral, and in violation of World Trade Organization (WTO) rules. Before its invasion of Ukraine and the resulting sanctions, Russia was the top exporter of the goods that will be covered by the CBAM (...). China was second and India was eighth. For these countries, the CBAM is a source of disruption and makes their exports into Europe less competitive. Brazil was 11th, just behind the United States.

Anyhow, CBAM pushes companies towards more sustainable practices, as occurs with ESG practices. ESG criteria are used by investors to evaluate the environmental impact, social responsibility, and governance of companies. Similarly, CBAM forces companies, especially those exporting to the EU, to account for the carbon footprint of their production.

This creates a direct link: businesses with better ESG practices, particularly those minimizing carbon emissions, tend to be less affected by CBAM.

f METHANE AND THE "BURP" TAX IN DENMARK

The first country to implement a carbon tax was Finland in 1990, as part of its efforts to reduce GHG emissions and combat climate change. This pioneering move marked the beginning of carbon pricing policies, which have since been adopted and adjusted by other countries around the world.

Finland's carbon tax initially covered fuels based on their carbon content, and over time, the tax was modified and expanded. This early adoption helped set the stage for other nations and regions to study related mechanisms, such as emissions trading systems and broader carbon pricing strategies.

A carbon tax is typically levied on fossil fuels or GHG emissions based on their carbon content. The government needs to decide the scope of the tax: which industries, activities, and types of emissions are covered. So, CO_2 is the typical villain in the climate change debate, as well as its emission using fossil fuels.

Less well recognized is the role that another GHG—methane—plays: because of its chemical configuration, methane triggers a far higher global warming potential than CO_2 (up to 80 times as much), while CO_2 is the primary driver of long-term climate change due to its abundance and longevity in the atmosphere, methane is much more harmful in the short term, making it a critical target for reducing near-term global warming. As explained by United Nations Environment Programme:[9]

> Methane is the primary contributor to the formation of ground-level ozone, a hazardous air pollutant and greenhouse gas, exposure to which causes 1 million premature deaths every year. Methane is also a powerful greenhouse gas. Over a 20-year period, it is 80 times more potent at warming than carbon dioxide.
>
> Methane has accounted for roughly 30 per cent of global warming since pre-industrial times and is proliferating faster than at any other time since record keeping began in the 1980s.

Scientists have been investigating how to reduce methane emissions and discovered that livestock is the largest emission source, responsible for 31% of the global total. By livestock, it means particularly ruminants like cows, sheep, and goats, that release methane primarily through a process called enteric fermentation, that happens during digestion and is a natural byproduct of how these animals break down food, particularly fibrous plant materials like grass.

Ruminants have a specialized digestive system with multiple stomach compartments, the largest being the rumen, where microorganisms (bacteria, protozoa, and fungi) help break down fibrous plant material that the animal eats. The methane that forms in the rumen is mostly released through the animal's mouth in the form of burping (eructation). This is the primary way methane escapes into the atmosphere from livestock.

Reducing methane emissions from livestock is considered a major step in solving agricultural contributions to global warming.

Science is making a lot of efforts to reduce this burden of methane, such as feeding livestock more digestible foods, such as grains or specially formulated feeds and adding substances to animal feed that can reduce methane production by inhibiting the methanogens in the rumen.

9. Methane emissions are driving climate change. Here's how to reduce them (unep.org), https://www.unep.org/news-and-stories/story/methane-emissions-are-driving-climate-change-heres-how-reduce-them#: ~ :text = Methane%20is%20a%20powerful%20greenhouse%20gas.

Massachusetts Institute of Technology has published an article properly named: "Methane research takes on new urgency at MIT," wherein it says:[10] "Researchers around the world are working on other dilute methane removal technologies. Projects include spraying iron salt aerosols into sea air where they react with natural chlorine or bromine radicals, thereby capturing methane. Most of these geoengineering solutions, however, are difficult to measure and would require massive scale to make a difference."

Harvard University has a similar approach and created a project named Harvard Initiative on Reducing Global Methane Emissions, based on the fact that:[11] "Methane-emissions abatement can, in the near term, significantly reduce the magnitude of climate change and its impacts—giving the world time to 'bend the curve' on CO_2 emissions, conduct research on carbon removal, and, more generally, to implement longer-term strategies to mitigate and adapt to climate change."

A company titled Lowercarbon capital, whose description is "Cows that burp less methane" developed a product named as Mootral Ruminant, that[12] "is a natural feed additive based on compounds from garlic and citrus extract. It reduces methane emissions by 30-38% while improving milk yield in dairy cows by 3-5%. Trials also point to reduced reliance on antibiotics and lower prevalence of cattle flies. The product is also 'Generally Recognized as Safe,' so it is in the market now and fits into existing supply chains."

Ok, science is trying to mitigate the harmful effects of methane emissions and taxation is also an useful tool for this specific challenge.

For example, the Inflation Reduction Act (IRA) of 2022 in the U.S. includes significant provisions aimed at addressing climate change, including the Methane Emissions Reduction Program, which directly imposes fees on methane emissions from the oil and gas sector. The program is administered by the Environmental Protection Agency (EPA) and focuses on cutting methane emissions from natural gas production, processing, transportation, and storage.

While the IRA's direct methane fees target the oil and gas sector, the law also includes provisions for agriculture by providing substantial funding through grants and incentives for farmers and ranchers to adopt methane-reducing technologies and practices. This includes support for anaerobic digesters, methane capture systems, and other innovations in manure management.

Specifically talking about taxation over cattle, Denmark will be the first country to implement a "burp tax": the idea behind this tax is to charge farmers for methane emissions based on the number of animals they own, particularly ruminants like cows and sheep and to use the generated revenue to fund research and development into

10. Methane research takes on new urgency at MIT | MIT News | Massachusetts Institute of Technology, https://news.mit.edu/2022/methane-research-takes-new-urgency-mit-1102#:~:text=One%20of%20the%20most%20notable%20climate%20change.
11. Harvard Initiative on Reducing Global Methane Emissions—The Salata Institute, https://salatainstitute.harvard.edu/methane-initiative-summary/#:~:text=The%20Harvard%20Initiative%20on%20Reducing.
12. Mootral | Lowercarbon Capital, https://lowercarboncapital.com/company/mootral/.

methane-reducing technologies, provide incentives for farmers to adopt more sustainable practices, or invest in green agricultural innovations.

According to CNN,[13] as published on June 27, 2024: "Dairy farmers in Denmark face having to pay an annual tax of 672 krone ($96) per cow for the planet-heating emissions they generate. The country's coalition government agreed this week to introduce the world's first carbon emissions tax on agriculture. It will mean new levies on livestock starting in 2030."

As this legislation will take some time to start being applicable, potential changes may happen, as some local farmers may argue, for example, that this tax policy would have to match EU legislation.

Therefore, science can work together with taxation to reduce carbon emissions by aligning scientific advancements with economic incentives for cleaner technologies and sustainable practices. However, taxation policies can penalize industries with high carbon footprints.

In any case, traditional energy models, industrial practices, and consumer habits have contributed substantially to global warming, and innovation is the key to transforming these sectors toward sustainability.

Thus, by harmonizing taxation with scientific innovation, governments can create economic conditions that drive businesses and individuals toward lower carbon footprints while science continually improves the tools and technologies needed to make significant reductions in emissions.

13. Denmark to charge USD 100 per cow in world's first carbon tax on farming | CNN Business, https://www.cnn.com/2024/06/26/business/denmark-cows-carbon-tax/index.html#: ~ :text = The%20tax,%20expected%20to%20be%20approved%20by.

CHAPTER 8
Innovation

a NEW IDEAS AND THE FIGHT AGAINST CLIMATE CHANGE

As discussed in Chapter 1 section e, continuous learning is a fundamental source of keeping our brains better and younger.

Curiosity drives people to seek out new information, learn about emerging trends, and explore unfamiliar fields. This continuous quest for knowledge is a critical component of the innovation process, as it enables individuals to stay informed about the latest developments and integrate diverse ideas into their work jointly with the exploration of new possibilities and the identification of areas where improvements or entirely new solutions are needed.

Curiosity not only drives individual learning but, when paired with diverse perspectives, can also lead to powerful innovations in addressing complex global issues like climate change.

Equally important, diversity plays a crucial role in encouraging innovation within organizations by bringing together a broad range of perspectives, experiences, and ideas. When teams are combined by individuals from diverse backgrounds—whether in terms of gender, age, culture, ethnicity, education, or life experiences—they are more likely to generate creative solutions, challenge conventional thinking, and drive innovation.

The focus on diversity within organizations aligns with the "Social" component of ESG, which emphasizes equitable practices, inclusivity, and community engagement. In homogeneous teams, there is a higher risk of "groupthink" when members conform to a single viewpoint to maintain their internal harmony.

Diversity helps to solve this conformity by encouraging dissenting opinions and boosting an environment where challenging the status quo is welcomed. Also, members learn from each other's experiences and expertise, which can lead to the development of new ideas and approaches that would not emerge in more homogeneous groups.

Even though there is some disagreement on this corporate movement towards innovation,[1] organizations that embrace diversity are more likely to develop innovative solutions, products, and services that meet the needs of a diverse and globalized world.

Johnson & Johnson, for instance, has long embraced diversity as a key factor in their business strategy. They maintain Employee Resource Groups that represent various racial, ethnic, and social groups, fostering an inclusive culture that develops innovation across product development. For example, their Band-Aid line expanded to include skin tones of various colors in response to customer feedback and the efforts of their diverse teams.

Another example is PepsiCo's: diversity and inclusion have been a significant driver of its innovative strategy. The company's diverse workforce led to the creation of new product lines, including healthier snacks like Baked Lays and innovations in sustainable packaging. Their Global Diversity and Engagement Council ensures that diversity continues as a top priority, driving product development and brand strategy.

Going beyond these punctual examples of innovative products, there is an urgent issue to be solved: climate change. Note most scientists believe the record-breaking temperatures, water scarcity, early hurricanes, wildfires, severe droughts, and sea level rise, along with many other indicators, show that the planet is warming fast and that all the heat-trapping emissions we release from burning fossil fuels are leading to this situation.

These environmental crises have underscored the urgency for innovation in technologies that reduce emissions and promote sustainable practices.

So, the time for action against climate change is now, and innovation is the key.

A crisis, while fundamentally challenging and disruptive, can bring several benefits, particularly in terms of growth, resilience, and creativity. Crises often force individuals, organizations, and societies to reevaluate current systems, assumptions, and routines. This can lead to significant changes that might have been resisted or delayed under normal circumstances.

When faced with a crisis, an urgent need for new solutions is frequent, driving innovation and creativity. Companies may develop new products, services, or ways of working to adapt to the changing environment.

For instance, the COVID-19 pandemic acted as a powerful catalyst for innovation across various industries and sectors, such as the spread of remote work and learning technologies, the rapid development of vaccines (particularly mRNA ones) and the popularization of telemedicine services.

Innovation is essential for creating technologies that reduce environmental impact, such as the development of renewable energy sources (solar, wind, bioenergy, geothermal, hydrogen) and energy-efficient appliances. These innovations help reduce reliance on fossil fuels, lower GHG emissions and consequently enable the movement to reach the limit established in the Paris Agreement.

---

1. The diversity backlash is underway. Here's how to resist it | World Economic Forum (weforum.org), https://www.weforum.org/agenda/2022/10/the-diversity-backlash-here-s-how-to-resist-it/.

Also, innovations in production processes, materials, and design can lead to more efficient use of natural resources. An example is next-generation solar cells made from perovskite materials that promise higher efficiency and lower production costs than traditional silicon-based cells. According to the Massachusetts Institute of Technology:[2]

> Perovskites hold promise for creating solar panels that could be easily deposited onto most surfaces, including flexible and textured ones. These materials would also be lightweight, cheap to produce, and as efficient as today's leading photovoltaic materials, which are mainly silicon. They're the subject of increasing research and investment, but companies looking to harness their potential do have to address some remaining hurdles before perovskite-based solar cells can be commercially competitive.

Revolutionary ultra-thin solar panels from perovskites can be portable, so they will be used as on-the-go to charge devices. This technology is tiny and flexible enough to apply to the surface of buildings, electronic gadgets, cars, or even clothing. Perovskite materials are being explored because they offer an efficient, cost-effective alternative to traditional solar cells, potentially transforming how we harness solar energy.

Expanding further, circular economy principles, which emphasize recycling, reuse, and minimizing waste, rely on innovative practices and technologies to close the loop between production and consumption. Companies are progressively focusing on eco-design, where products are constructed with their entire lifecycle in mind, minimizing environmental impact from production to disposal. Innovations in materials science, such as the development of biodegradable plastics or alternative materials, are key to this process.

Day by day, new technologies are developed and launched by highly known companies.

Honeywell, the giant industrial products, solutions and technologies company, announced the release of "INNCOM Direct," a new tool focused on mid-market hotels to reduce energy consumption and carbon emissions by automatically regulating heating and cooling of empty rooms.

It is made through a detection system to identify empty spaces and to set temperature without impacting consumer comfort. It can change temperature in a room if a guest leaves for an extended time and simply readjust when the guest returns. Billal Hammoud, President and Chief Executive Officer of Honeywell Building Automation, said:[3]

> As hotels become more carbon-conscious, they are taking meaningful steps to show they care about their impact on the environment. Until now, mid-market hotels faced fewer options when it came to better managing their HVAC systems

2. Explained: Why perovskites could take solar cells to new heights | MIT News | Massachusetts Institute of Technology, https://news.mit.edu/2022/perovskites-solar-cells-explained-0715.
3. Honeywell Launches INNCOM Direct to Help Mid-Market Hotels Reduce Their Carbon Footprint, https://www.honeywell.com/us/en/press/2024/08/honeywell-launches-inncom-direct-to-help-mid-market-hotels-reduce-their-carbon-footprint.

> with automation. Now, INNCOM Direct is leveling the playing field with an affordable, cloud-based energy management system.

So, this smart system reduces unnecessary energy consumption, thus decreasing GHG emissions from heating or cooling mechanisms located at mid-market hotel buildings.

Further than this example of automation to help improve energy efficiency, another one comes from Nespresso: after three years of research and development, the company released home-compostable espresso pods. This fact represents a turning point for the company, especially in the context of increased scrutiny regarding the environmental impact of its single-use aluminum capsules.

Additionally, innovations in agriculture, such as precision farming, rational irrigation and genetically modified crops, can increase food production while reducing the environmental footprint, conserving water, and minimizing the use of chemical inputs. Regenerative agriculture can reverse soil degradation, increase carbon sequestration, and reduce the need for chemical inputs, leading to more resilient and productive farming systems.

A specific challenge for the agricultural industry is to reduce methane, a particularly dirty GHG (already commented about in the chapter about "the burp tax"), that in its vast majority is released from cattle "enteric" emissions, or cow burps.

Researchers around the world are studying possibilities to reduce this methane emission from cattle: adding algae, seaweed or certain synthetic compounds to cattle feed can change the chemical reactions that generate methane and to inhibit the enzymes in the stomach that produce it, leading to a significant reduction in emissions.

Also, data analytics technologies use sensors, cameras, and other monitoring tools to track the health and behavior of cattle. By analyzing data on feeding patterns, digestion, emissions and other factors, farmers and researchers can optimize nutrient composition and management practices to reduce methane emissions.

An innovative tactic to address this topic is the production of meatless meat (plant-based or lab-grown meat), as it has the potential to reduce the need for livestock farming, which in turn reduces methane emissions. Meatless meat is promoted as a more sustainable option because it not only reduces methane emissions but also conserves water and land resources.

These technologies and approaches are part of a wider effort to make livestock farming more sustainable and environmentally friendly. By reducing methane emissions, the agricultural sector can contribute notably to global climate change mitigation goals.

Sustainability challenges create opportunities for innovation, while innovation provides the tools and solutions needed to achieve SDGs. This symbiotic relationship is crucial for addressing global challenges like climate change, resource depletion, and social inequality.

And it requires collaboration between different sectors—public, private, academic, and nonprofit. Policies that promote renewable energy, energy efficiency, and sustainable practices encourage businesses to innovate in these areas.

b THE WAY TAXES SUPPORT INNOVATION

Governments around the world are realizing that fiscal policies, including taxation, are powerful tools to incentivize businesses and individuals to invest in innovative solutions that address environmental challenges. They can provide economic measures and policy initiatives aimed at promoting environmental sustainability and combating climate change through government spending, incentives, and regulations.

Green agenda stimulus policies can speed economic growth while preventing environmental degradation, biodiversity loss and depletion of natural resources. These initiatives often involve substantial investments in green technologies, renewable energy, sustainable infrastructure, and other environmentally friendly practices. The goal is to stimulate economic growth while simultaneously addressing environmental challenges.

Moreover, governments and private companies can form partnerships to fund, develop, and manage green projects, such as renewable energy infrastructure, sustainable transport systems, and energy-efficient buildings.

Collaboration between government and the private sector is crucial for advancing the green agenda. By leveraging each other's strengths—governmental policy, regulation, and incentives alongside private sector innovation, capital, and efficiency—these partnerships can drive significant progress toward environmental sustainability.

This cooperation not only addresses immediate environmental challenges but also fosters long-term economic growth and societal well-being. Achieving a successful green agenda requires ongoing dialogue, shared goals, business-oriented visions and a commitment to sustainable development from both public and private sectors.

Taxation plays a vital role in this, as Tax Authorities may grant financial incentives for businesses and individuals to invest in research and development (R&D), adopt new technologies, and engage in creative problem solving. These are the most habitual ways in which tax policies are used to stimulate innovation:

(1) Direct Incentives for Innovation: R&D tax credits can reduce the effective cost of research and development activities for businesses. By allowing companies to deduct a portion of their R&D expenses from their tax liabilities, these credits make it more financially viable for firms to invest in innovation. This encourages businesses to undertake more research, develop new products, and improve existing ones. Note that in some jurisdictions, it is possible to obtain an extra deductible expense as a premium for development of new science. In China, for example, companies can deduct 150% of the cost of R&D equipment from their taxable income in the year the equipment is purchased.

(2) Tax Deductions for Innovation-Related Investments: Permitting businesses to deduct the costs of acquiring new technology, machinery, or software that enhances productivity or enables innovation can encourage firms to modernize and innovate, extending it to the creation and protection of IP, such as

patents, trademarks, and copyrights. Canada, for example, has the Accelerated Investment Incentive, that allows businesses to write off a larger share of the cost of new capital investments in the year they are made, which can include investments in innovation-related machinery and equipment.

(3) Reduced Tax Rates on IP Income: Some countries implement "patent box" regimes, where income derived from patents and other forms of IP is taxed at a lower rate when compared with other commercial revenues. In Europe, for instance, 13 of the 27 EU Member States currently have a patent box regime in place. This encourages companies to innovate and develop new technologies, knowing that profits from these innovations will be taxed at a favorable rate, and it is aimed at incentivizing not just large multinational corporations but also SMEs to invest in innovation and hold their patents domestically.

(4) Tax Incentives for Startups: Tax relief for investors who fund startups and early-stage companies can enhance the availability of capital for innovative ventures. Governments can offer tax breaks on capital gains from investments in startups, making it more attractive to participate in high-risk, high-reward innovation. Israel, for instance, provides a Tax credit for individual investors who capitalize on an early-stage Israeli R&D company (not surprisingly, technology is responsible for more than 50% of local export revenues). In some countries, startups and small businesses can receive payroll tax credits for R&D activities, allowing them to offset payroll taxes instead of income taxes. India has a tax holiday on profits system for startups for three consecutive years out of their first 10 years of operation, provided they meet certain criteria.

(5) Incentives for Collaboration between Industry and Academia: Tax incentives for businesses that collaborate with universities and research institutions can promote the exchange of knowledge and drive innovation. These partnerships often lead to the development of cutting-edge technologies and solutions. Canada has a very advanced program about this, the Scientific Research and Experimental Development Tax Incentive Program, "that offers tax incentives to over 20,000 organizations annually, totalling about $4.2 billion that help Canadian businesses fund their research and development projects."[4] Belgium has the Flanders Cleantech Cluster that offers a specific personal income withholding tax of 80% reduction for researchers in certain scientific fields.

(6) Tax-Advantaged Zones: Establishing Special Economic Zones or innovation hubs with tax advantages, such as reduced corporate taxes, exemptions on import duties for R&D equipment, and other incentives, can attract innovative companies to cluster in specific regions, fostering a collaborative environment that spurs innovation. Some remarkable examples of Special Economic

4. The SR&ED landscape in Canada—KPMG Canada, https://kpmg.com/ca/en/home/insights/2024/07/the-sr-ed-landscape-in-canada.html.

Zones include China's Shenzhen Special Economic Zone and Singapore's Jurong Island. Special Economic Zones are a great vehicle for international trade and FDI to drive economic development, as they ensure investors financial incentives as well as a proper infrastructure (e.g., seaports and airports).

(7) Tax Policy Stability and Certainty: Providing stable and predictable tax policies that support innovation over the long term allows businesses to plan their R&D investments with greater confidence. Uncertainty in tax policies can deter companies from investing in long-term innovation projects, so it is quite common that investors and host states define stabilization clauses addressing how to deal with potential changes in tax law in the host state during the life of the project. One of the most usual deals occurs through "freezing clauses," wherein legislation implemented after the date of the agreement does not apply to the foreign investors or the project unless the investors agree. These clauses freeze the tax regime at the time of signing. For example, if the corporate tax rate is 20% when the investment contract is signed, it will continue at 20% for the investor, despite any future increase.

Tax policies that minimize the financial barriers to innovation, reward risk-taking, and incentivize collaboration can significantly promote new science towards a more sustainable future. By creating a supportive tax environment, governments can work together with the private and academic sectors to encourage businesses and individuals to invest in new ideas, technologies, and processes, ultimately driving economic growth and competitiveness.

And this is a reality for one of the protagonists when talking about clean energy: green hydrogen, an abundant, renewable, and nonpolluting source of energy that will possibly become the "new oil" within the next years.

c A RISING STAR FOR ENERGY TRANSITION: GREEN HYDROGEN

Hydrogen is the most abundant chemical element on Earth, present in 75% of all matter on the planet. Nevertheless, this element is never found alone but in the company of other chemical elements, such as oxygen composing water or carbon forming other organic compounds, such as hydrocarbons.

Green hydrogen is produced by electrolyzing water using renewable energy sources such as wind or solar power. Electrolysis is a process that utilizes electrical energy to split water molecules into hydrogen and oxygen gases. When this process is powered by renewable energy, it can be used to create green hydrogen.

It is a clean fuel that can be used in various sectors, including transportation, industry, and energy storage and has the potential to decarbonize hard-to-electrify sectors such as heavy industry and long-distance transport, contributing to significant reductions in global GHG emissions.

In an appropriately named article, "Why green hydrogen could play a major role in powering our sustainable future," the World Economic Forum describes it as the potential fuel of the future, as follows:[5]

> Hydrogen, the simplest and most abundant element in the universe, has the potential to be the fuel of the future. It's an energy carrier that can store and deliver energy in a usable form. In its pure form, hydrogen is a colourless, odourless and non-toxic gas. It's high in energy, yet an engine that burns pure hydrogen produces almost no pollution, making it a desirable source of power.
>
> (...) hydrogen holds immense potential as a sustainable energy carrier. While there are challenges to overcome, particularly in terms of cost and infrastructure, the benefits of hydrogen in terms of sustainability and versatility make it a key player in the global energy transition. As we continue to innovate and improve hydrogen production methods and as the cost of renewable and nuclear energy continues to fall, the role of green and pink hydrogen in our energy system is set to grow.

While green hydrogen offers significant environmental benefits, particularly in lowering carbon emissions, it also comes with challenges and potential negative effects.

These drawbacks primarily relate to production, storage, distribution, and use of green hydrogen. Hydrogen has a low energy density by volume, requiring it to be stored under high pressure or at very low temperatures (as a cryogenic liquid).

Also, transporting hydrogen, whether by pipeline, truck, or ship, requires specialized infrastructure that is not widely available. Finally, another barrier to be removed is the reduction in the price of production methods for "green" hydrogen to compete with kerosene, as its production is dependent on the availability of renewable energy. Variability in renewable energy generation (e.g., solar and wind power) can impact the consistency of production.

So, current green hydrogen methods are not easily scalable to meet global energy demands and expanding its production capacity requires overcoming technological, logistical, and economic hurdles.

In any event, these challenges create new ideas on how to circumvent them.

As an example, Brazil's ethanol, a liquid fuel derived from sugarcane, used to successfully move Brazilian vehicle engines for at least four decades, may be utilized as an energy source to produce green hydrogen especially. Note Brazil has a well-established ethanol production and distribution infrastructure, which can be leveraged to develop a hydrogen economy. Ethanol can be transported and processed at existing facilities, reducing the need for new infrastructure investments.

Also, Brazil's energy matrix is heavily reliant on renewable energy sources, such as hydropower. Integrating ethanol-based hydrogen production with renewable electricity (for electrolysis) can create a highly sustainable energy system. Royal Dutch Shell, for instance, is keenly investing in developing technology that converts ethanol

5. Hydrogen is a key fuel for our sustainable future | World Economic Forum (weforum.org), https://www.weforum.org/agenda/2023/12/why-hydrogen-is-the-fuel-of-the-sustainable-future/.

into green hydrogen ethanol and green hydrogen production through a partnership with Raízen, a major biofuels player, and other institutions like the University of São Paulo and SENAI CETIQT.

In addition, in the EU, green hydrogen producers may benefit from the EU ETS by earning carbon credits that can be sold to other companies needing to offset their emissions. Also, the framework named "European Green Deal" has a special attention to green hydrogen.

Expectedly, tax administrations around the world are starting to regulate the "new oil." South Korea, for example, is delivering ambitious plans to become a leader in the development of hydrogen projects. Its Hydrogen Economy Roadmap includes tax incentives for companies that invest in green hydrogen production and infrastructure. These incentives include corporate tax reductions, accelerated depreciation for hydrogen-related assets, and exemptions from certain import duties on equipment used in hydrogen production.

Germany—still a heavy user of fossil fuels, that correspond to something around 75% of its energy source—is also moving rapidly toward cleaner sources and provides several tax incentives and financial support measures to promote green hydrogen production as part of its broader energy transition strategy.

Germany's key incentives include lower electricity taxes for green hydrogen producers when using renewable energy sources for electrolysis, making production more cost-competitive and also local government provides significant grants and subsidies for research, development, and deployment of hydrogen technologies under programs like the National Hydrogen Strategy.

Besides these examples above, other tax administrations around the world are granting benefits to green hydrogen, and this reflects the reality of governments boosting clean new oil. An article in May 2024 in Forbes Magazine reflects this thought as follows:[6]

> It means that taxation or subsidies will still be needed to attract the private sector in the current decade as the market enters a pivotal phase. But a dynamic mix of tax incentives, subsidies and private sector investment may just propel the green hydrogen industry to a trillion-dollar business by the turn of the decade.

The relevant regulation bringing incentives for the green economy for the U.S. is the IRA, signed in August 2022. It introduces, for example, a new production tax credit under section 45V for "qualified clean hydrogen" produced after 2022. The credit offers up to USD 3 per kilogram of hydrogen produced, depending on the lifecycle carbon emissions of the hydrogen production process.

Also, IRA allocates funding for the development of regional hydrogen hubs, which are designated areas where the production, storage, and end-use of hydrogen are

6. State Incentives or Free Markets: How to Drive the Hydrogen Economy Forward? (forbes.com), https://www.forbes.com/sites/gauravsharma/2024/05/14/taxation-subsidies-or-free-markets-how-to-drive-the-hydrogen-economy-forward/.

concentrated. These hubs are expected to drive economies of scale, encourage collaboration between public and private entities, and help develop necessary infrastructure for green hydrogen.

Moreover, IRA provides significant financial incentives and regulatory support for green hydrogen through production and investment tax credits, funding for infrastructure and innovation, and market development initiatives. These measures lower the cost of green hydrogen production, encourage the deployment of related technologies, and create demand across multiple sectors, helping to accelerate the transition to a low-carbon economy.

Note the IRA is a landmark for the "green tax" legislation aimed at addressing several major challenges, including inflation, climate change, healthcare costs, and tax fairness. The IRA represents the most significant federal investment in climate action in U.S. history (it allocated nearly USD 370 billion through a series of tax credits, loans, grants and subsidies) while also providing measures to reduce healthcare costs and promote tax equity.

And this is a new reality for governments all around the world: to use tax tools to open space for the development of new ideas towards decarbonization.

d OIL MAJORS MOVING TOWARDS GREEN HYDROGEN

The prospects are so positive for this new energy source that in 2022, the European Commission released the European Hydrogen Bank. This mechanism aims to create investment security and business opportunities for green hydrogen production. It is not designed to be a physical institution but is a financing instrument run internally by European Commission services.

The funding comes from the Innovation Fund, which gets its revenues from the EU's carbon market. It has EUR 800 million available, and companies must submit their production plans and those with the lowest costs will be awarded the money. This fund's purpose is to reduce its prices by subsidizing production, paying a part of the bill for every kilogram of hydrogen produced.

Going deeper into this, several major oil companies are shifting towards green hydrogen production as a relevant part of their broader strategy to transition to cleaner energy sources (such as solar, wind, and carbon capture technologies) and to reduce carbon emissions.

An example of a recent operation involving a company in this industry was the billionaire investment made by Brookfield Asset Management on a company that works with efuels—ultra-low carbon synthetic fuels—named Infinium, that advocates these fuels as[7] "are created using waste CO_2 and green hydrogen derived from renewable power. We actively partner with leading renewable energy producers around the world as well as companies seeking beneficial reuse solutions for their carbon waste."

7. Infinium Ultra-low Carbon eFuels (infiniumco.com), https://www.infiniumco.com/.

Brookfield plans to invest up to USD 1.1 billion in Infinium, focusing on sustainable aviation fuel (SAF); SAF is a critical topic for several causes related to reducing GHG emissions, meeting regulatory and market demands, enhancing energy security, and driving economic growth in a sustainable way. Note the aviation sector is a substantial contributor to global GHG emissions, accounting for approximately 2-3 % of global CO_2 emissions and 12 % of CO_2 emissions from all transport sources.

Continued research, development, and investment in SAF technologies will be indispensable to scale production, reduce costs, and increase adoption across the aviation industry. Brookfield is aware of this, and such investment will support Infinium's "Project Roadrunner," a power-to-liquid e-fuel production plant in Texas, and other e-fuel projects globally.

Furthermore, the fossil fuel divestment movement is expanding towards this emerging source of energy and here is how some of the most prominent oil companies in the world are actively investing in green hydrogen:

- Saudi Aramco, the world's largest oil producer, is exploring green hydrogen production as part of Saudi Arabia's broader Vision 2030 initiative. The company is involved in the NEOM project, a futuristic USD 500 billion city being built from scratch in the northwest of the country, which aims to produce large quantities of green hydrogen using solar and wind energy.
- Equinor, the giant Norwegian oil company, is expanding its renewable energy portfolio to include green hydrogen. The company is involved in the H2H Saltend project in the U.K, which aims to produce low-carbon hydrogen, with plans to transition to green hydrogen using renewable energy in the future. As explained by the company on its website:[8] "This project represents a bold but practical first step towards delivering the world's first net zero industrial cluster by 2040. This unparalleled project can play a leading role in the UK's journey to net zero by 2050, renew the UK's largest industrial cluster, and unlock technology that will put the UK at the forefront of a global hydrogen economy."
- Repsol, a Spanish oil company, is actively pursuing green hydrogen as part of its goal to achieve net-zero emissions by 2050. The company has launched several green hydrogen projects, including a partnership with Enagás to develop green hydrogen production at its industrial complexes in Spain. Repsol is also involved in the SHYNE (Spanish Hydrogen Network) project, the biggest multisectoral consortium in Spain around renewable hydrogen.
- Shell Royal Dutch, the global group of energy and petrochemicals, is substantially investing in green hydrogen as part of its broader energy transition strategy. The company is involved in the NortH2 project in the Netherlands, which aims to produce green hydrogen using wind energy from the North Sea. The project is one of the largest of its kind and could produce up to 10 gigawatts of green hydrogen by 2040. The company is also developing

8. H2H Saltend—Equinor, https://www.equinor.com/energy/h2h-saltend.

hydrogen refueling stations and exploring the use of green hydrogen in various industrial applications, such as refining and chemicals.

- TotalEnergies is diversifying its energy portfolio with investments in green hydrogen. The company is part of the HyDeal Ambition project, which aims to produce green hydrogen at a competitive price in Europe by 2030. HyDeal projects website manifests that: "Hydrogen can replace coal, oil and natural gas in virtually all applications, turning heavily polluting and CO2 emitting industries into clean and zero-carbon ones."[9] This project involves several partners and focuses on using solar energy to produce hydrogen.
- PetroChina started in July 2024 the construction of its first green hydrogen production plant in Xinjiang. The facility, with a production capacity of 20,000 tons per year is aligned with the Chinese government's efforts to develop green infrastructure, as the country plans to utilize its massive generation capacity in renewable energy.
- Chevron, a major player in the petroleum industry, is beginning to explore green hydrogen as part of its strategy to transition to lower carbon energy. The company has invested in hydrogen technologies and is looking into the potential for green hydrogen production in the U.S. and other regions. The company announced in February 2024 its first solar-to-hydrogen production project in California's Central Valley.
- BP (the former British Petroleum) and Iberdrola have formed a 50:50 joint venture to develop a 25MW green hydrogen project. It is expected to avoid the emission of 23,000 tons of CO_2 per year. The project, expected to be operational by 2026, will use renewable energy from Iberdrola's wind and solar power plants to produce green hydrogen. Besides this project, the two companies are planning to develop their green hydrogen production capabilities in Spain, Portugal, and the U.K.

As can be perceived, oil majors, traditionally focused on fossil fuel extraction and production, are increasingly positioning themselves as broader energy companies with a developing focus on clean and renewable energy. This transition is complex and varies among companies in terms of commitment, scale, and speed, but it is worthwhile to notice these significant movements towards integrating cleaner energy into their portfolios.

Investing and innovating in green hydrogen is experiencing extraordinary momentum and companies and industries are dedicating time and efforts to understand how this zero-emission energy source can apply as an essential factor in their net-zero climate strategies. As these huge corporations do this, it affects competition, pricing, and the future development of hydrogen as a robust energy source.

Aviation industry, for example, is a major contributor to global GHG emissions. Green hydrogen is increasingly being considered a potential alternative to conventional aviation fuels, even though some challenges related to storage, infrastructure, cost, and

9. HyDeal, https://www.hydeal.com/.

technology need to be addressed before it can become a widespread solution. As defined by Airbus on its website:[10]

> If progress on the hydrogen economy's ramp-up continues as expected, green hydrogen will not only be readily available but also cost-effective by 2030—a timeline that aligns with Airbus' ambitions. Indeed, Airbus fully expects green hydrogen to power its future zero-emission aircraft when it reaches the market by 2035. The green hydrogen ecosystem for aviation is already taking shape as more and more key players sign on to make it a reality. The challenge today is to support long-term scale-up to ensure there is enough green hydrogen available to fuel the aviation industry's needs.

Continued research, investment, and innovation will be critical to overcoming these barriers and realizing the potential of green hydrogen, not only in aviation but also for the whole economy.

And the governments shall be part of this plan by necessarily involving the use of taxation tools to encourage investments in innovation.

e FASHION INDUSTRY AND ITS CONTRIBUTION TO INNOVATIVE PRACTICES

Companies can reduce carbon emissions through various strategies focused on energy efficiency, renewable energy, sustainable practices, and carbon offsetting.

A lot of attention from investors interested in ESG impact investment has been directed to the textile industry, and it includes not only production itself but also labor practices, air and water pollution, responsible use of resources, and brand reputation.

Note the textile industry relies heavily on energy-intensive processes such as spinning, weaving, dyeing, and finishing, which often use fossil fuels. This triggers considerable CO_2 emissions. And the production of synthetic fibers, like polyester and nylon, which are derived from petroleum, is highly energy-intensive and emits significant amounts of CO_2. Polyester, the most widely used fiber, emits almost three times more carbon emissions than cotton.

Its waste, like unsold inventory, production scraps, and post-consumer waste, all contribute to landfill and incineration waste. When textiles, especially synthetic ones, are landfilled, they can release methane, a toxic GHG. With millions of tons of textiles ending up in landfills annually, this contributes significantly to GHG emissions. Besides this, plastics used in synthetic fibers are deposited in the oceans and turn into microplastics that contaminate fauna (as these animals mistake the scent of plastic for food, it triggers the classic and sad image of turtles in agony).

Also, the production of textiles, mostly cotton, needs large amounts of water. For example, it can take up to 2,700 liters of water to produce a single cotton T-shirt. This extensive water use contributes to water scarcity, which is exacerbated by climate change.

10. The green hydrogen ecosystem for aviation, explained | Airbus, https://www.airbus.com/en/newsroom/news/2021-06-the-green-hydrogen-ecosystem-for-aviation-explained.

As published by the European Parliament website:[11]

> Fashion is the second most polluting industry in the world, coming just after oil. Clothing manufacture and consumption have a huge negative impact on both the environment and people. Sustainability is not only about the environment, but is also an economic and social indicator, and the clothing industry is a good example illustrating their interconnections.

So, as textile industry has long been known as a big polluter, there is an urgency to become sustainable, to improve workers' safety (along with its supply chains) and to ensure the right of consumers to make adequate choices, especially in times of "fast fashion," which usually lead to overproduction and overconsumption.

Aiming to achieve the proper path to sustainable practice, there is an increasing effort adopted by the textile industry to mitigate carbon emissions by adopting sustainable practices, improving energy efficiency, and transitioning to eco-friendly materials and processes. Here are some key strategies and examples:

(1) The utilization of sustainable materials: eco-friendly fibers such as bamboo, hemp, or recycled materials instead of conventional cotton or synthetic fibers can lead to a lower carbon footprint and require less water and chemicals.

(2) Improve energy efficiency in production: the upgrade of technologies, such as low-liquor dyeing, digital printing, and waterless dyeing techniques, which consume less energy and water can be more environmentally friendly, as well as the implementation of energy management systems to monitor and optimize energy consumption in production processes.

(3) Minimize water use and wastewater emissions: by adopting closed-loop water systems, water recycling technologies and advanced wastewater treatment systems to remove pollutants and reuse water in the production process. Also, opt for nontoxic, biodegradable dyes and chemicals to minimize pollution and the carbon footprint of textile processing.

(4) Adoption of circular economy practices: boost the recycling of old textiles and garments into new products (for example, through the creation of programs for consumers to return used garments for recycling), reducing the demand for virgin materials while creating durable, high-quality products designed to last longer, reducing the overall need for new production. Also, it is advisable to minimize production waste by optimizing cutting patterns, repurposing offcuts, and recycling scrap materials. This idea of circular economy means that products are designed to make it easier to recycle and reclaim their materials at the product's end-of-life.

(5) Optimize supply chain and logistics: Manufacture closer to markets to reduce transportation emissions and improve transportation efficiency using fuel-efficient or electric vehicles for transport and optimize shipping routes to minimize fuel consumption.

11. What if fashion were good for the planet? (europa.eu), https://www.europarl.europa.eu/RegData/etudes/ATAG/2020/656296/EPRS_ATA(2020)656296_EN.pdf.

(6) Adopt digital tools: use digital technologies such as 3D modeling and virtual sampling to minimize the need for physical samples and minimize waste. Also, to analyze production data to recognize areas of inefficiency and to optimize processes for lower energy use and waste, as well as reduce inventory.

Again, the textile industry significantly affects climate change due to its high carbon footprint and resource-intensive processes. It contributes to GHG emissions, water pollution, and waste, all of which exacerbate environmental degradation and climate change.

Cotton farming, for example, is associated with significant deforestation, especially in areas where new farmland is created by clearing forests. This contributes to the loss of carbon sinks, which are critical for mitigating climate change. Moreover, the use of agrochemicals and intensive farming techniques in the cultivation of natural fibers like cotton can lead to soil degradation, reducing the land's ability to sequester carbon.

However, there is hope for a brighter future for the textile industry, and it lies in innovation, as is occurring for the oil industry.

And an interesting example of an idea for fashion industry was created by a startup based in Brazil and Boston, U.S., named Galy, a biotech company that focuses on producing lab-grown cotton by applying cellular agriculture technology. Instead of cultivating cotton in fields, Galy grows cotton fibers in a lab environment by using plant cells. This innovative approach aims to generate a more sustainable alternative to traditional cotton production. The process takes place in this manner:[12]

> To create its first product, Literally Cotton, Galy places cells from cotton plants in tanks called "bioreactors." By precisely controlling the conditions inside the bioreactor, Galy coaxes the cells into growing into cotton fibers that can then be harvested, dried, and used like any other cotton.
>
> According to Galy, this process uses 80% less water than traditional cotton production, and because it takes place in a lab, there's no need for pesticides or insecticides. Production can also happen year round and under any weather conditions, helping keep costs and yields stable.

This concept has a positive prospect and has just obtained USD 33 million funding from Bill Gates' Breakthrough Energy Ventures, H&M, and Inditex (whose company's flagship brand is Zara).[13]

Addressing the impact of the textile industry is essential because of its extensive contribution to global carbon emissions and its role in various forms of environmental degradation. Reducing their carbon footprint can help slow down climate change and

12. Lab-grown cotton is on its way to consumers (freethink.com), https://www.freethink.com/science/lab-grown-cotton.
13. GALY Raises USD 33M From Bill Gates' BEV, H&M, and Inditex to Advance Climate-Resilient Cultivated Cotton—vegconomist—the vegan business magazine, https://vegconomist.com/investments-finance/galy-raises-33m-from-bill-gates-bev-hm-and-inditex-to-advance-climate-resilient-cultivated-cotton/.

create a more sustainable future and the idea behind Galy seems appropriate to this purpose.

Innovation plays an important role and brings an ikigai not only to the scientists working with this but also to the tax professionals who will frame these new ideas into the tax incentives established for this new mindset.

And it is applicable not only to the textile industry but also to the whole innovation environment we are facing today as a global effort towards decarbonization.

CHAPTER 9

The Outlook for ESG and Tax Integration

a CONSOLIDATION OF ESG FACTORS INTO TAX AND REGULATORY POLICY

Environmental, Social, and Governance (ESG) factors intersect with a broad range of disciplines, from economics and law to sociology, engineering, and behavioral sciences. This intersection creates a holistic approach to tackling global challenges like climate change, social inequality, and corporate ethics. Integrating ESG into multiple areas of knowledge helps build more sustainable, equitable, and resilient societies.

In economics, for example, ESG factors are increasingly used to assess long-term risks and opportunities, shaping how companies are valued and how capital is allocated. ESG is considered when studying consumer behavior, such as the growing demand for sustainable products and services or the willingness to pay a premium for goods from socially responsible companies.

The incorporation of ESG aspects into models that evaluate the externalities of economic activities includes analyzing the costs of pollution, carbon emissions, or social inequality and incorporating these factors into national accounts, corporate balance sheets, or economic policies.

Also, ESG considerations are reshaping supply chain strategies to minimize environmental impacts, ensure ethical labor practices, and manage governance risks. This includes adopting sustainable sourcing practices, reducing carbon footprints, and increasing transparency and accountability all over the supply chain.

The EU Supply Chain Directive (CSDDD) commits companies to achieve their responsibilities throughout the supply chain by trying to mitigate suppliers' adverse impact on human rights and the environment, comprising (but not limited to) slavery, child labor, pollution or destruction of natural heritage and biodiversity.

CSDDD is a rich example of how ESG factors influence laws and regulations related to environmental protection, labor rights, corporate governance, and anti-corruption.

So, there is an evolving landscape of ESG-related litigation and the role of legal frameworks in promoting corporate responsibility.

Additionally, as seen in the previous chapter, ESG principles drive the development of technologies and engineering practices that minimize environmental impact, such as the development of cleaner technologies, renewable energy systems, green infrastructure, and sustainable manufacturing processes that align with green agenda goals and the promotion of innovation that directly contributes to social well-being and equitable development.

ESG pillars are pivotal to developing public policies on issues like climate change, social equity, and corporate transparency. Tax policies, such as progressive taxation, can play a crucial role in addressing these inequalities and financing early interventions in marginalized communities, for example, the number 10 (reduction of inequalities), whose purpose is defined by the United Nations International Children's Emergency Fund (UNICEF) as:[1]

> Goal 10 aims to reduce inequality within and among countries. Inequality starts with the lottery of birth—who your parents are and where you are born—that accounts for variation in the resources and opportunities available to people. The social and economic inequalities and disadvantages in early life can limit opportunities for the realization of one's rights and the ability to realize one's full potential. Discrimination based on age, gender, ethnic or racial group, disability status, sexual orientation, migratory status, residence or other factors serve to disadvantage some individuals in many different and often invisible ways, throughout their lives. These patterns of inequality get passed on from generation to generation. Therefore, early interventions and investing in all children, especially the poorest and most marginalized, is central to breaking intergenerational poverty and inequality. Achieving Goal 10 and the SDGs more broadly requires a deliberate strategy to reach the furthest behind, first.

Also, ESG foundations are progressively being integrated into tax policy frameworks by governments and organizations aiming to promote sustainability, social responsibility, and ethical governance in plenty of ways, as follows:

- Green Investment Incentives: Tax credits, deductions, or accelerated depreciation rates for investments in renewable energy, recycling activities, energy-efficient technologies, or environmentally sustainable practices boost businesses to adopt greener strategies.
- Resource Taxes: Taxes on the extraction or use of natural resources (like minerals, water, or fossil fuels) encourage sustainable resource management and reduction of waste. Resource taxes directly refer to the "E" in ESG by encouraging businesses and individuals to use resources more efficiently. For example, a tax on water extraction stimulates companies to adopt water-saving technologies, while a carbon tax (directed to foster lower carbon emissions by enforcing taxes on carbon-intensive activities) drives investments in renewable energy and energy efficiency.

1. SDG Goal 10: Reduced Inequalities—UNICEF DATA, https://data.unicef.org/sdgs/goal-10-reduced-inequalities/.

- Incentives for Socially Responsible Practices: Tax credits may be provided for companies that invest in community development, education, health, and other social welfare programs. This includes deductions for charitable donations or tax incentives for companies that provide culture sponsorship, good working conditions, and employee benefits. Or tax exemptions commonly granted to nonprofit organizations—that evidently rely on some criteria, like having organized accountability and operating exclusively for charitable purposes.
- Taxes on Negative Social Externalities: Taxes on products and services that have negative social effects, such as tobacco, alcohol, or sugary drinks, aim to reduce their consumption and improve public health results. However, lowering or eliminating taxes on essential goods and services (for example, food, medicine, and education) aids low-income households and promotes social equity.

An integrated and interdisciplinary tax policy approach, reached through collaboration across government departments, including finance, environment, social welfare, and development, ensures that tax policies are aligned with broader national and international sustainability goals, just like reducing poverty, improving public health, and advancing education.

This holistic approach is complex, as it requires careful balancing of multiple goals, including revenue generation, economic growth, social equity, and environmental protection, which can sometimes conflict. However, it is a powerful tool for promoting sustainable development, encouraging equitable growth, and encouraging responsible corporate behavior through the integration of insights from multiple disciplines.

b TAX TECHNOLOGY

Tax technology refers to the use of digital tools, software, and technological solutions to automate, rationalize, simplify, and enhance various aspects of tax administration, compliance, planning, and reporting. It encompasses a broad range of technologies, including data analytics, AI, machine learning, blockchain, cloud computing, and robotic process automation, which are applied to improve the efficiency, accuracy, and effectiveness of tax-related processes. Within this concept, there are some relevant tools, such as:

- Tax compliance software is designed to help businesses and individuals comply with tax laws and regulations, track tax regulations through many countries, and ponder different thresholds for regulation, registration, tax rates, reporting and returns required. These tools automate the preparation and filing of tax returns, calculate tax liabilities, and manage payments.
- Data analytics and reporting tools that leverage data analytics and business intelligence to provide insights into tax-related data. They help organizations

identify tax risks and opportunities for tax optimization and guarantee compliance with intricate tax regulations.
- Robotics process automation that includes using software robots (bots) to automate repetitive, rule-based tasks in tax processes, namely data entry, reconciliation, and validation.
- Blockchain technology is planned for a secure, transparent, and immutable ledger for recording transactions, which can be used for tax administration and compliance.
- Cloud-based platforms supply scalable, secure, and cost-effective solutions for tax management, thus allowing real-time collaboration, data storage, and access from anywhere.
- Digital reporting (or "e-Invoicing"), which comprises the digital generation, exchange, and processing of invoices between suppliers and buyers, which is substantially being mandated by tax authorities worldwide.

Tax technology leads to cost savings for both businesses and tax authorities. Also, advanced tools like AI and machine learning can identify patterns and incongruities in tax data, helping tax authorities and companies to identify and mitigate risks of tax evasion or avoidance.

Therefore, it helps to minimize human errors in tax calculations and data entry, ensuring more accurate tax filings and reducing the risk of penalties due to noncompliance.

The relationship between tax technology and ESG derives from the need for transparency, accountability, efficiency, and sustainability in both tax management and expansive corporate governance. By enhancing transparency, promoting fair tax practices and enabling better data management, tax technology helps companies align their tax strategies with their broader ESG commitments. In other words, by sharing it among the letters of the ESG acronym:

- Environmental: Advanced analytics tools can analyze large datasets to assess the environmental impact of different business activities. This information can be used to optimize supply chains, reduce waste, and lower carbon emissions, aligning tax practices with environmental sustainability objectives. Also, it can track and report on compliance with environmental regulations, like emissions limits or resource use caps. This ensures that companies are adhering to policies aimed at reducing their environmental footprint, thus contributing to broader environmental sustainability goals.
- Social: Tax technology assists companies to adhere to fair tax practices by promoting compliance with tax laws across jurisdictions. By automating tax calculations and reporting, companies can avoid aggressive tax avoidance schemes that undermine social equity. This aligns with the "social" aspect of ESG, which includes fair contributions to the communities and societies in which companies operate. In addition, an efficient tax collection accelerated by technology increases government revenues, which can be allocated to

social programs such as education, healthcare, and infrastructure. This supports the achievement of social development goals and ensures that businesses contribute fairly to the rendering of public services.

- Governance: Transparent tax practices, enabled by technology, build trust and credibility with stakeholders, including employees, customers, investors, the community around them, and regulators. This is important for maintaining a positive social license to operate and demonstrating a commitment to ethical and socially responsible behavior. This aligns with governance principles by reducing chances for tax evasion, corruption, and fraud, making certain that companies are more accountable for their tax practices. Moreover, technologies like blockchain construct immutable records of transactions, providing a clear audit trail that develops accountability and compliance. This is particularly useful in demonstrating responsible governance practices in ESG reporting.

As published by PWC in a properly named study called "Why Digital Technology is Critical to ESG Success":[2]

> Digital technologies are already being used to improve efficiency, reduce waste and provide less carbon-intensive means of environmental management. ESG frameworks, in turn, can help organizations apply a broader approach to sustainability and highlight the potential risks in applying new digital technologies. For example, they have a social impact in the form of job displacement and reduced human-to-human contact.
>
> Changing the way we use digital technology can significantly move the dial, such as by embedding ESG metrics as part of the technology sourcing processes and introducing electronic waste management. It can also play a central role in enabling an organization's governance through systems that provide improved transparency, decision-making capabilities, and empowerment of compliance.
>
> Digital technology is the key component of an ESG strategy, but it is also clear that an ESG-focused mindset can help organizations approach it in a sustainable, thoughtful way.

Of course, it is not that simple to implement it, as it can require significant upfront investment in software, hardware, and training. The adoption of tax technology requires a workforce skilled in data analytics, software development, and digital tools. A lack of expertise in these areas can hinder the effective use of tax technology. Integrating these technologies with existing systems can also be tricky.

Another challenge results from handling sensitive taxpayer information digitally, which increases the risk of data breaches and cyberattacks. Guaranteeing strong cybersecurity measures and compliance with data protection regulations is decisive.

Tax technology supports more efficient financial planning and resource allocation by providing accurate data on tax liabilities, incentives, and credits related to ESG initiatives, including renewable energy projects or R&D in green technologies. This

2. Why Digital Technology Is Critical to ESG Success (pwc.com), https://www.pwc.com/m1/en/media-centre/articles/why-digital-technology-is-critical-to-esg-success.html.

allows companies to optimize their tax positions while aligning their financial strategies with sustainability goals.

So, despite challenges associated with data security, high costs, and regulatory complexity, the potential benefits make tax technology an indispensable tool for businesses aiming to achieve long-term sustainable growth and to encounter the expectations of investors, regulators, and other stakeholders.

c EXECUTIVE COMPENSATION LINKED TO ESG PERFORMANCE

ESG backlash is a real phenomenon.

In recent years, there has been growing criticism and resistance against the adoption and integration of ESG factors in business practices, investment strategies, and regulatory policies. This backlash comes from various stakeholders, including some politicians, businesses, investors, and interest groups, who argue that businesses and investors should focus solely on financial performance rather than becoming involved in social or political issues.

The topic has become a politically charged issue, markedly in the U.S. Some politicians claim that ESG concerns can interfere with free-market principles, lead to regulatory overreach, or reflect a political agenda that prioritizes certain social and environmental goals over economic growth and profit itself. Several states have proposed or enacted laws to restrict state investments in funds or companies that use ESG criteria.

From a corporate standpoint, some businesses consider ESG requirements as onerous, costly, or a potential threat to their core operations and profitability. There is apprehension that ESG considerations will impose new regulations, reporting requirements, or operational changes that do not align with a company's business focus or industry needs.

In any case, while there is tangible and developing resistance to ESG practices, this backlash could ultimately lead to more mature, robust, and credible ESG frameworks that better balance social, environmental, and financial goals. So, there is a spreading drive for standardization and clearer guidelines. Organizations like the ISSB and the GRI are working to determine standardized ESG reporting frameworks to improve comparability, consistency, and transparency.

Also, regulatory support for ESG disclosure and integration is growing worldwide. The EU, for example, has implemented several regulatory frameworks, like the SFDR and the CSRD, demanding more transparency and standardization in ESG reporting.

In addition, in March 2024, the U.S. Securities and Exchange Commission (SEC) published rules to develop and standardize climate-related disclosures by public companies and in public offerings, aiming to make public SEC's efforts to answer to investors' demand for more trustable and consistent data about the financial consequences of climate-related risks on a registrant's procedures and how these risks are managed.

Among the data required to be presented under these recent SEC regulations, companies shall disclose Greenhouse Gas Emissions Reporting, aiming to provide a fuller picture of a company's carbon footprint. Moreover, if a company has set climate-related targets or goals, it must release details about those goals, including the time frame, progress, and methodology used to achieve them.

Certainly, this U.S. movement (that has already been similarly implemented in many countries) towards a real ESG disclosure will bring more light to a growing phenomenon: to link executive's compensation to ESG performance.

It is happening first because ESG metrics are viewed as leading indicators of future financial performance and potential risks, as leaders are incentivized to consider the broader impacts of their decisions, which can lead to more thoughtful, balanced, and sustainable strategies, thus discouraging short-term thinking and risky behavior aimed solely at increasing short-term profits.

In the same way, companies can foster innovative approaches to sustainability challenges, like thinking about new products or services that reduce environmental impact or improve social effects and improve efficiency—such as reducing energy use, creating strategies for rational use of water, minimizing waste, or optimizing supply chains—which can trigger cost savings and increased profitability over time.

Furthermore, companies are more likely to avoid practices that could lead to reputational damage, in particular environmental violations, poor labor conditions, or governance scandals. Strong ESG performance can help build a positive corporate image and mitigate risks associated with negative publicity. Similarly, employees tend to feel engaged and committed when they believe their organization is contributing positively to society and the environment.

This explains why, according to research published by Semler Brossy consulting firm,[3] "72% of S&P 500 companies applied ESG in incentive plans this year, representing a net 2.8% year-to-year growth in companies using ESG metrics vs. 23% growth last year."

Also, as per this study, "Carbon footprint and energy efficiency metrics continue to have the largest year-over year increases among environmental metrics as both have emerged as the environmental metrics of choice in the sample. Both metrics are top-of-mind to investors and often work in conjunction together to push companies towards the overall goal of operating with more sustainable energy usage."

Among other examples of companies linking ESG goals to pay executives compensation, Nestlé, one of the world's largest food and beverage companies, has linked executive compensation to a range of ESG factors to drive progress toward its sustainability and social goals. In accordance with its 2023 compensation report:[4]

> For the CEO and the CFO, 85% of the target is linked to performance against the Nestlé Group objectives (see below) and 15% to Environmental, Social and

3. 2023 ESG + Incentives Reports—Semler Brossy, https://semlerbrossy.com/insights/2023-esg-incentives-reports/.
4. Boardreport_2023_en.indd (nestle.com), https://www.nestle.com/sites/default/files/2023-03/agm-2023-board-directors-report-en.pdf.

> Governance (ESG) objectives. For the other members of the Executive Board, at least 35 % of the target is linked to business performance, to ensure accountability for Nestlé's results, for Function Heads, 50 % is tied to functional objectives, 35 % to Group performance and 15 % to ESG objectives; for Zone or Business Heads, 60 % is tied to business objectives they are directly responsible for, 25 % to Group performance and 15 % to ESG objectives.
>
> ESG objectives (15 % of the target) are set annually by the Compensation Committee and reflect selected performance measures from the Company's ESG/Sustainability agenda. For 2023, they relate to affordable nutrition with micro nutrients, reduction of greenhouse gas emissions, plastic packaging designed for recycling, reduction of water use in factories and management positions held by women. These five objectives are equally weighted at 3 % each.

Another giant corporation in the food and beverage industry, Danone's executive compensation is linked to company's commitment to becoming a certified B Corporation and its "One Planet, One Health" sustainability framework. The compensation metrics include targets for reducing carbon emissions, increasing sustainable agriculture practices, and advancing biodiversity. By integrating these ESG metrics, Danone ensures that executives are financially motivated to meet the company's sustainability objectives.

In the pharmaceutical industry, Novartis is an example of a company which has added ESG metrics to its executive pay structure, particularly in relation to access to medicines in low-income countries, fostering ethical business practices, and reducing the environmental impact of its operations. These ESG goals are part of the long-term incentive plan for its leadership team.

As executive compensation increasingly includes ESG performance metrics, companies may develop tax strategies to align with these ESG-linked incentives. This could involve structuring compensation in ways that optimize tax efficiency while encouraging long-term sustainable performance.

Observe that executive compensation is generally tax-deductible for the company, but there are often limits on how much can be deducted, particularly for highly paid executives. In the U.S., for example, section 162(m) of the Internal Revenue Code limits the deductibility of executive compensation paid by publicly traded companies to their top executives. The rule allows only up to USD 1 million per year to be deducted for each of the CEO, CFO, and some other highest-paid officers.[5]

Similarly, when executive compensation is tied to ESG goals that align with government policy objectives (like reducing carbon emissions or enhancing innovation), companies may find themselves better positioned to take advantage of tax benefits or grants made available for these initiatives. This association can make ESG-linked compensation more financially valuable from a tax perspective.

5. "In the case of any publicly held corporation, no deduction shall be allowed under this chapter for applicable employee remuneration with respect to any covered employee to the extent that the amount of such remuneration for the taxable year with respect to such employee exceeds $1,000,000."

d TAX ROAD TO SUSTAINABLE DEVELOPMENT AND TRANSPARENCY

The "tax road to sustainable development" involves using tax policies and incentives to promote sustainability, reduce environmental impact, and achieve the United Nations SDGs. Governments and organizations increasingly recognize that tax systems can be a powerful mechanism for driving sustainable development by influencing behavior, encouraging investment in green technologies, and supporting social equity.

As ESG considerations become more central to business strategy and regulatory frameworks, the integration of tax policies with ESG objectives is expected to intensify. Shareholders are likely to continue pushing for greater transparency around both ESG and tax practices. This could result in more shareholder resolutions demanding disclosure of tax practices, contributions to public revenue, and alignment with SDGs. Companies may face growing pressure to explain how their tax strategies support their ESG objectives.

This movement also aligns with the Global Reporting Initiative 207 (GRI 207), which emphasizes the importance of tax transparency. As noted by GRI Director of Capital Markets, Dave Reubzaet:[6]

> Sometimes it seems like everyone—governments, investors, civil society—is talking about tax. And with good reason! Taxes play a key role in funding national and global priorities, reducing inequality, and financing the low-carbon transition. Fundamentally, the world cannot address the collective sustainability challenges we face without tax.
>
> Investors, in particular, regard tax transparency as a highly relevant topic when it comes to their reporting expectations for companies. That is why consistent and comparable reporting—at the country-by-country level—is needed, as enabled by GRI 207. This is about ensuring that tax is an "engine for good," positively contributing toward socio-economic cohesion, environmental value, and long-term prosperity.

With growing scrutiny from tax authorities and regulators, companies may need to ensure their tax strategies align with their ESG commitments. Businesses that engage in aggressive tax avoidance might face reputational risks and decrease investor confidence, especially as stakeholders demand greater corporate responsibility and transparency.

As KPMG puts it, "tax transparency is here to stay":[7]

> Tax transparency is here to stay. There has been a paradigm shift in the global tax landscape, resulting in public and political pressure to tackle perceived harmful

6. GRI—How taxes demonstrate impact and accountability (globalreporting.org), https://www.globalreporting.org/news/news-center/how-taxes-demonstrate-impact-and-accountability/#:~:text=%E2%80%9CSometimes%20it%20seems%20like%20everyone%20%E2%80%93%20governments,%20investors.
7. Tax transparency is here to stay (kpmg.com), https://kpmg.com/xx/en/our-insights/eu-tax/tax-transparency-is-here-to-stay.html#:~:text=Tax%20transparency%20is%20here%20to%20stay.%20As%20anyone.

> tax practices, particularly by corporate entities. Information reported under existing "non-public" Country-by-Country Reporting (CbCR) requirements helps tax authorities gain a better understanding of multinational corporations' tax profiles and structures. However, institutions such as the EU are also introducing "public" CbCR rules to ensure public accountability and promote more informed public debate around tax compliance.

Furthermore, the KPMG Responsible Tax project focuses on "involves engaging in the debate on tax, looking to build consensus and understanding between business, decision-makers and civil society in a constructive and transparent way to help ensure outcomes are seen to be fair and effective."[8]

This debate is also central to the work of The B Team, the global nonprofit initiative promoting a new way of doing business that balances financial success with environmental sustainability, social responsibility, and ethical governance. The B Team advocates for responsible tax principles and emphasizes the role of tax compliance in building trust and contributing to sustainable development:[9]

> Complying with tax rules is core to business responsibility. Businesses have a fundamental responsibility to comply with tax legislation in every country they operate in, paying the right amount of tax at the right time. Over recent years, the tax affairs of major businesses have been subject to unprecedented levels of scrutiny and controversy. In some cases, there has been confusion where public expectations do not align with the design of the tax system. In other cases, there has been justified concern over aggressive tax avoidance practices. To meet stakeholder expectations, build trust, and contribute to informed public debate, businesses must proactively manage their tax affairs responsibly and explain their tax practices and results. This will encourage the development of more effective and transparent tax systems.

Being tax responsible is not only a corporate issue but also a governmental one. Macroeconomic policies, especially tax policies, offer significant support to carbon emission reduction goals and sustainable development. Tax revenues from carbon taxes or other environmental levies can be used to fund retraining programs, support vulnerable communities, and ensure that the benefits of the transition to a low-carbon economy are broadly shared.

This reflects the concept of a "just transition," which aims to ensure that the shift to a green economy is fair and inclusive, especially for workers and communities impacted by the phase out of fossil fuels.

The OECD's 2024 edition of "Tax Policy Reforms: OECD and Selected Partner Economies"[10] highlights the increasing role of environmentally related taxes in tax policy:

8. KPMG Responsible Tax, https://responsibletax.kpmg.com/content/why-responsible-tax.
9. The B Team | The B Team Responsible Tax Principles: Accountability, https://www.bteam.org/our-thinking/reports/the-b-team-responsible-tax-principles-accountability-report-2024#:~:text=Companies%20that%20sign%20up%20to%20The%20B%20Team.
10. OECD (2024), *Tax Policy Reforms 2024: OECD and Selected Partner Economies*, OECD Publishing, Paris, https://doi.org/10.1787/c3686f5e-en.

> Over the past decade, environmentally related taxes have become more central to tax policy, both as a means to incentivize the transition towards environmental sustainability and as a source of revenue. These taxes encompass levies on tax bases of particular environmental relevance, such as agrochemicals, energy, road use, vehicles, waste, and water pollution. Well-designed environmental taxation systems can influence environmental outcomes by encouraging businesses and households to consider the environmental costs of their behaviors, thus favoring greener economic activities.

The Tax for SDGs Initiative, led by the United Nations Development Programme (UNDP) and supported by the governments of Finland and Norway, seeks to help countries align their tax systems with the SDGs. The initiative promotes the use of tax policy as both a revenue-raising tool and a means of encouraging sustainable growth, addressing areas such as climate action, gender equality, and good governance.

Policymakers must carefully design tax policies to avoid unintended consequences. New tax measures linked to ESG goals should not disproportionately impact lower-income households or marginalized communities.

Looking forward, the integration of ESG and tax policies will likely involve stronger alignment between tax tools and sustainable development objectives. This will require using taxation to promote environmental sustainability, social equity, and good governance while ensuring transparency, accountability, and international cooperation.

As businesses, investors, the media, and policymakers increasingly recognize the importance of integrating ESG factors into tax strategies, we can expect continued innovation and evolution in this space.

e THE FUTURE IS GREEN AND DIGITAL

The Industrial Revolution has left lasting effects on the modern world, laying the foundation for contemporary industry, technology, and economic structures. It was a turning point in human history, accelerating economic growth, increasing productivity, and transforming societies on a global scale. However, it also introduced challenges such as labor exploitation and environmental degradation, issues that remain relevant today.

The effects of the Industrial Revolution have been a central part of this book, especially when discussing the origins of anthropogenic carbon emissions and large-scale deforestation, as trees were cleared to expand mining operations and accommodate growing industrial cities. We also explored the role of the Luddites, who revolted against the new labor machinery.

The Industrial Revolution began in the United Kingdom in the late 1700s and spread to other countries in Europe, North America, and eventually across the globe.

Coal was one of the most important fuels of this era, powering key industries and technological advancements. It was essential for steam engines, which became drivers of industry and transportation. Coal-powered steam engines in factories, locomotives, ships, and pumps revolutionized both industry and transportation.

The rise of railroads was another major development during the Industrial Revolution, with coal serving as the primary fuel for steam locomotives. Railroads revolutionized the transportation of raw materials, goods, and people, creating unprecedented connectivity between industrial centers. Additionally, coal-fueled ships expanded global trade and the movement of goods.

But today, another revolution is taking place.

On September 30, 2024, Britain became the first G7 country to end coal-fired power production. The U.K. has officially discontinued using coal for electricity generation, offsetting this decline by significantly increasing its use of renewable energy, particularly wind and solar power. The U.K. is now a global leader in offshore wind energy, with renewable sources becoming a dominant part of its energy mix.

Energy minister Michael Shanks remarked, "The era of coal might be ending, but a new age of good energy jobs for our country is just beginning."[11]

This is particularly remarkable given Britain's historical significance as the world's first coal-fired economy, which helped it become an industrial powerhouse in the 19th century. Notably, taxation has played an important role in this transition, with the imposition of a carbon tax on power generators making coal less competitive than cleaner alternatives like natural gas and renewables.

China, another giant economy, is also moving toward clean energy on an ambitious and transformative path. As the world's largest emitter of GHGs, China has recognized the need to transition to cleaner energy sources. China has set significant targets to reduce its reliance on fossil fuels, particularly coal, while rapidly expanding its renewable energy capacity.

China is now a global leader in renewable energy investment, consistently outspending other countries. In 2022 alone, China invested over USD 546 billion in energy transition technologies, accounting for nearly half of global investment in renewables. This is part of its 14th Five-Year Plan (2021-2025) and reflects broader efforts to reduce dependency on coal, which still accounts for around 56% of China's energy consumption.

Germany is another prominent example of a major economy committed to phasing out coal. The country has set a target to phase out coal by 2038, with pressure to accelerate this deadline to 2030. Germany's "Energiewende" (energy transition) policy focuses on shifting from fossil fuels and nuclear power to renewable energy sources like wind and solar. The government is providing significant financial support to coal-dependent regions to ease the transition. Renewable energy already accounts for a large share of Germany's power mix.

Additionally, the country provides subsidies and tax relief for investments in renewable energy infrastructure and energy-efficient technologies like solar panels and electric vehicles. Germany is also implementing a carbon pricing system for heating

11. Britain to become first G7 country to end coal power as last plant closes | Reuters, https://www.reuters.com/sustainability/climate-energy/britain-become-first-g7-country-end-coal-power-last-plant-closes-2024-09-29/#:~:text=Britain%20will%20become%20the%20first%20G7%20country%20to.

and transportation fuels, which taxes emissions. This tax increases the cost of fossil fuels, making renewables more competitive and reducing overall emissions.

Many other countries are offering similar incentives, focusing on energy transition, with strong support from taxation policies. There is a global recognition of the urgency of climate change and the necessity to act toward sustainable living. Movements advocating zero waste, ethical consumption, and conservation of natural resources are gaining momentum.

The future is green and digital.

From an environmental perspective, AI can help model climate scenarios, optimize renewable energy sources, and monitor deforestation and biodiversity loss. AI-powered systems can enhance energy efficiency in industries and buildings, reducing carbon emissions. Additionally, AI can optimize farming practices by analyzing soil data, weather patterns, and crop health, leading to more efficient use of water, pesticides, and fertilizers, ultimately increasing food production while reducing environmental impact.

In healthcare, AI and machine learning algorithms have made great developments in medical imaging, diagnostics, and drug discovery. AI models now rival or surpass human experts in detecting diseases such as lung cancer, breast cancer, and diabetic retinopathy from medical scans. AI will continue to revolutionize early disease detection, helping diagnose conditions more accurately and faster than ever before. It is also speeding up the development of new drugs by analyzing vast amounts of biological data, predicting outcomes, identifying drug candidates, and optimizing clinical trials.

This progress inspires optimism for a better future.

Continued advancements in medicine, such as new treatments and vaccines, promise to improve quality of life and extend lifespans. The rapid development of mRNA vaccines during the COVID-19 pandemic demonstrated the potential of this technology to combat infectious diseases. Additionally, regenerative medicine, including stem cell therapies, has made significant progress in treating conditions like spinal cord injuries, heart disease, and neurodegenerative disorders. Scientists are also successfully growing tissues and organs in labs, offering hope for transplant advancements.

Other breakthroughs, such as 3D printing, wearable health technology, personalized medicine, and anti-aging research, promise to transform healthcare even further. Biomimicry—where solutions are inspired by nature, like the creation of Velcro, inspired by the way burdock burrs stick to animal fur—is also gaining traction in fields like engineering and medicine.

From a social perspective, the past century has seen significant progress in human rights recognition and protection. Movements for gender equality, racial justice, and LGBTQ+ rights continue to push for a more inclusive society. Moreover, increased access to education, particularly in developing countries, is empowering individuals and lifting communities out of poverty.

Victor Frankl believed that humans have an inherent drive to find purpose. The fight against climate change, environmental degradation, and social inequalities is a powerful example of global adversity that offers individuals the opportunity to find meaning in their work. As people engage in efforts to solve these massive challenges, they often experience a profound sense of meaning, knowing they are contributing to something larger than themselves.

As the world moves toward a green economy, new opportunities are emerging for jobs and industries focused on sustainability. This shift presents opportunities for economic growth that benefit both people and the planet, which also aligns beautifully with the idea of "ikigai."

Taxation can be a powerful tool in this process, helping to turn the world into a greener and more innovative future. By incentivizing sustainable practices, funding research in green technologies, and redistributing resources to support a low-carbon economy, tax policies can accelerate the transition to a more sustainable and environmentally friendly world.

With careful design, these policies can drive innovation, create jobs, and ensure the benefits of a green economy are shared equitably across society. So, tax is a relevant key to addressing inequality, incentivizing sustainable practices, promoting public services, and funding innovation.

Taxation is a powerful tool for creating a fairer, healthier, and more sustainable world.

Conclusion: Ozone Layer Recovery, Reasons to Believe in a Better Future and Noah's Rainbow

As a kid who grew up in the 1980s, I was alarmed about three different matters that were trending topics at that time: (1) the Cold War and its potential nuclear war consequences; (2) the dissemination of HIV cases; and (3) the hole in the ozone layer. According to the news, these three factors, together or separately, would somehow impose the end of life on Earth.

The first item was imploded in 1989. Of course, other wars succeeded, but the widespread risk of a nuclear war was theoretically far away. The other two were mitigated by the evolution of science. As this is not a book about public health, I will not digress about the successful therapies to hold HIV.

However, this book has a lot to do with environmental science, so it is important to understand the debates about the recovery of the ozone layer and the lessons to be learned about it.

First, ozone works as Earth's protective shield against damaging ultraviolet (UV) radiation from the sun. A thinner ozone layer allows more UV-B radiation to reach the Earth's surface, increasing the risk of skin cancer, cataracts, and other health issues. It also impacts ecosystems, particularly marine life, as UV radiation can harm plankton and disrupt the food chain. This means we need high ozone concentrations in the stratosphere to guarantee that Earth's inhabitants are not exposed to harmful concentrations of UV-B radiation, which can damage and disrupt DNA.

The depletion of the ozone layer was discovered in the mid-1980s, primarily through satellite data and ground-based observations. Such discovery of the "ozone hole" led to a global alarm and extra-scientific investigation confirmed the relationship between human-made chemicals, especially chlorofluorocarbons (CFCs), and the degradation of the ozone layer. These substances—at that time, widely used in refrigerants, aerosol sprays, cooling devices and industrial solvents—emit chlorine and bromine when they reach the stratosphere, and these elements break down ozone molecules through complex chemical reactions.

As this dramatic news was published, worries sounded around the world and the projections demonstrating that the destruction of the ozone layer would harmfully impact the life of humans and ecosystems sparked public fear, boosted scientific investigation and stimulated the world's governments to collaborate in an unprecedented way.

Then, an international treaty was adopted in 1987, the Montreal Protocol. This treaty targeted to phase out the production and consumption of CFCs, which were widely used at that time. According to the United Nations Environmental Program:[1]

> The Montreal Protocol on Substances that Deplete the Ozone Layer is the landmark multilateral environmental agreement that regulates the production and consumption of nearly 100 man-made chemicals referred to as ozone depleting substances (ODS). When released into the atmosphere, those chemicals damage the stratospheric ozone layer, Earth's protective shield that protects humans and the environment from harmful levels of ultraviolet radiation from the sun. Adopted on 16 September 1987, the Protocol is to date one of the rare treaties to achieve universal ratification.

Since the Montreal Protocol effectively came into effect, levels of CFCs and other harmful chemicals in the atmosphere have decreased drastically and this fact has allowed the ozone layer to begin a slow process of healing. According to NASA and the World Meteorological Organization, as the ozone layer is slowly recovering, the Antarctic ozone hole, which was a major environmental concern in the 1980s, is shrinking, and scientists project that the ozone layer could return to pre-1980 levels by around 2060, depending on the region.

Therefore, the ozone layer is recovering due to coordinated global action under the Montreal Protocol, which successfully phased out many harmful substances. Nevertheless, continued vigilance is required to guarantee recovery remains on track, especially in the face of emerging challenges.

The successful Montreal Protocol offers several key lessons that can be applied in the fight against climate change, as its success in addressing the depletion of the ozone layer provides valuable insights into how global environmental challenges can be tackled effectively.

And one of the most important lessons is the necessity of global cooperation: the Montreal agreement was universally ratified, meaning all countries, both developed and developing, worked together to phase out ozone-depleting substances. Similarly, addressing climate change requires a unified global effort where all nations contribute according to their abilities, since climate change is a global issue.

A significant characteristic of the Montreal Protocol was the establishment of a Multilateral Fund to assist developing nations in the transition away from ozone-depleting substances, ensuring that poorer nations had the financial and technological support necessary to comply with the agreement. An analogous approach is needed in climate change mitigation and adaptation: rich nations shall support developing

1. About Montreal Protocol (unep.org), https://www.unep.org/ozonaction/who-we-are/about-montreal-protocol#:~:text=The%20Montreal%20Protocol%EE%80%80%20on%20Substances%20that.

countries through financial aid, technology transfer, and efforts to help them reduce emissions.

Another important lesson taught by the Montreal Protocol is the imposition of gradual targets to alleviate the use of ozone-depleting substances, thus allowing industries to adjust and innovate without abrupt economic shocks. Evidently, this phased approach also stimulated science through the development of alternatives to harmful chemicals, which created a competitive market for ozone-friendly products, pushing companies to innovate more quickly and adopt sustainable practices.

Climate policy must take a comparable approach by setting clear timelines for phasing out fossil fuels while encouraging innovation in clean energy technologies. And taxation is crucial for this, as economic incentives like carbon pricing or incentives for renewable energy and innovation can help guide industries toward sustainable practices.

Back in the 1980s, many countries implemented taxes or duties on ozone-depleting substances to discourage their use and make alternatives more attractive. These taxes made it financially unrealistic for companies to continue using harmful chemicals, as well as encouraging industries to transition to environmentally friendly alternatives. An example is the tax imposed on CFCs by the U.S. under the Clean Air Act, making their continued use more costly for industries. This tax, known as the "CFC Tax," progressively increased over time to discourage production and consumption. This tax not only helped reduce CFC usage by making alternatives more financially viable but also generated revenue that could be used to fund environmental protection programs.

So, taxation had a pivotal role in bringing good news for the recovery of the ozone layer.

In the climate change arena, the contemporary alignment between government and private sector towards global energy transition trends gives us practical reasons to hope for a better future. From a historical perspective, it is impressive how much progress has been made in an incredibly short period of time.

Talking about a historical outlook (a lot more ancient than the concerns present in a 1980s kid head), in the Book of Genesis (Chapters 6-9), the Creator noted that human beings had become sinful and violent, filling the Earth with corruption. To cleanse the world of this wickedness, G-d decided to send a flood that would destroy all living creatures.

However, there was a righteous and blameless man: Noah. So, the Creator instructed Noah to build an ark to save himself, his family, and two of every kind of animal (male and female) from the imminent flood. Then, Noah was able to survive the flood, preserving life on Earth to start again once the floodwaters retreated.

And the receded of the floodwaters brought a symbol to the sky: a rainbow. In the biblical story of Noah, the rainbow holds a significant meaning, being introduced as a sign of the pact between the Divine and humanity, as well as all living creatures on Earth.

The rainbow, therefore, symbolizes hope and the renewal of life after the destruction of the flood and a sign that the water will never cover Earth again. We tend to forget that this mutual covenant was established not only between the Creator and

Noah but with all future generations (as Genesis 9:13 says: "My rainbow I have placed in the cloud, and it shall be for a sign of a covenant between Myself and the earth").

As a result, we, the Eternal's creations, are required to do our part to keep that covenant alive and work for a better, more peaceful world.

And the "ark" symbolizes the efforts to save the planet and its ecosystems, encouraging proactive measures to mitigate future environmental disasters through sustainable practices, cooperation (despite political convictions), and the reduction of carbon footprints, taking us to a new rainbow.

It marks a new beginning for Noah, his family, and all living creatures, signifying that life will continue and flourish once more.

Noah's Ark serves as a powerful metaphor in environmental discourse, emphasizing themes of preservation, moral responsibility, preparedness, and global cooperation—key elements of the Green Agenda, that focuses on protecting and preserving the environment to prevent ecological catastrophes such as climate change, biodiversity loss, and environmental degradation.

And climate change is both one of the biggest challenges of our times and a significant opportunity for transformation and innovation. The urgency of addressing climate change presents wide-ranging impacts on the environment, economies, and societies. Overall, the efforts to combat climate change also raise immense opportunities for businesses, governments, and individuals to rethink how we operate and build a fairer future.

Therefore, climate change is an extraordinary challenge, but it also presents one of the most significant opportunities for transformation and innovation in modern history. As the world deals with the threats posed by a warming planet, it is also fostering a shift towards cleaner technologies, sustainable practices, and systemic change, unlocking new economic, social, and technological opportunities that will shape the future.

This crisis is driving humanity to rethink how we live, work, and grow, ultimately driving us toward a more sustainable and resilient world.

www.ingramcontent.com/pod-product-compliance
Ingram Content Group UK Ltd.
Pitfield, Milton Keynes, MK11 3LW, UK
UKHW020821290926
15470UKWH00003B/1297

9 789403 506098